A Time for Peace

*Daily Meditations
for Twelve-Step Living*

Mary Ylvisaker Nilsen

Illustrated by Kristi Ylvisaker
Edited by R. Cheryl Friedman

ZION PUBLISHING

A Time for Peace:
Daily Meditations for Twelve-Step Living

Copyright 1990 by Mary Ylvisaker Nilsen. All rights reserved. No portion of this book may be reproduced in any form, except for brief quotations in reviews, without written permission from the publisher.

The Twelve Steps are reprinted with permission of Alcoholics Anonymous World Services, Inc. Permission to reprint and adapt the Twelve Steps does not mean that AA has reviewed or approved the contents of this publication, nor that AA agrees with the views expressed herein. AA is a program of recovery from alcoholism only. Use of the Twelve Steps in connection with programs which are patterned after AA but which address other problems does not imply otherwise.

Scripture quotations contained herein are adapted from the King James Translation, RSV, TEV, or JPS.

Library of Congress Catalog Card Number: 90-90177

For ordering information, call
Zion Publishing
1-800-996-2777

ISBN 0-9627147-0-4
Zion Publishing
Iowa City, Iowa

Printed in the United States of America

PRINTED ON RECYCLED PAPER
Third Printing

January 1

Create in me a pure heart, O God, and put a new and steadfast spirit in me. PSALM 51:10

"Create in me. . . ." We long for a pure heart and a new spirit. We deeply desire to be free from all that oppresses our inner selves: our angers, fears, hates, resentments; our intolerance and self-righteousness; our impatience and ingratitude; our unhealthy attachments and our addictions. We have struggled in many ways to achieve this newness, often with mixed results.

Now, this day, the first day of the year, we turn to God and ask for something new. We plead for an act of creation within us. And we are promised that God will work with us, creating and renewing. God wants us to be free from all of the inner constraints and restraints that choke off real living. It is God's will for us that we be able to love and be loved, to bear and be borne. Whatever the outer circumstances of our lives, God can work on our inner self, creating a pure heart and putting a new and steadfast spirit in us.

May God's creative work continue in our hearts and lives.

January 2

Let me hear the sounds of joy and gladness. PSALM 51:8

What are the sounds of joy and gladness? We know the loud sound of rage or the dissonant sound of frustration. We recognize the plaintive sigh of resignation or the deep sigh of unfulfilled longing. We have heard the clamor of need—people, often those we love, expecting, asking, demanding, draining us dry. Noise presses in on us like a vice clamped to our souls. But, the most terrifying sound of all can be the sound of silence—the silence of emptiness, the silence of loneliness, the silence of God.

But the psalmist prays for a new sound, the sound of joy and gladness. Was he praying for ears that could hear it or for the presence of such sounds? Either way, he knew that being able to receive good sounds helps to lighten our spirits and lift our souls; sounds such as the laughter of a child, beautiful music, the chatter of friends; a voice bringing good news; sounds that reassure us of the presence and goodness of God.

May God fill our hearts with the sounds of joy.

January 3

I am worn out, O Lord; have pity on me! Give me strength; I am completely exhausted. PSALM 6:2

How often have we not wept like the psalmist, feelings of exhaustion pressing us down, sapping us of strength, leaving us unable to handle even the simple tasks of the day.

The Twelve Steps toward spiritual renewal begin here. We face our lack of strength and our powerlessness over people and events in our lives. We acknowledge that there is much in our own lives over which we have no control. It is often painfully difficult to admit that we cannot change other people or most events. And it is even harder to admit that our own lives are out of control. But the road to spiritual recovery and maturity begins at this point – when we are worn out from trying, exhausted from taking on problems and expending enormous energy in an effort to solve them. The wonderful news of the First Step is that while we are powerless, God is not. We can quit spinning our wheels. We can relax in the assurance that our lives and the lives of those we love are in much stronger hands than our own.

May our Deliverer release us from all that exhausts our bodies and spirits.

January 4

The Lord is a haven for the oppressed, a place of safety in times of trouble. PSALM 9:9

Oppression stalks us like a thief in the night trying to rob us of our freedom. Sometimes oppression comes from without—institutions, legal systems, political or social enemies working against our well-being. Or oppression might come from living with a chemically dependent person. Surely it comes from our own addictions—those compulsions over which we seem to have no control.

Even more insidious are the subtle oppressors of the spirit that come disguised: self-righteousness, self-pity, resentment, guilt, anger, shame. The Second Step toward spiritual recovery is the process of coming to believe that God can save us from all our oppressors. In biblical times, travelers along narrow paths could easily be attacked and destroyed because their vision was obstructed. "Salvation" was reaching the wide open places, the safe places, where vision was not limited, where oppressors could be recognized and faced. God is our refuge, our safety, our wide open place.

May God create for us wide open places in our lives.

January 5

Proverbs... help you recognize wisdom and good advice and understand sayings with deep meaning.
PROVERBS 1:2

Like people rushing to the scene of a tragedy, so advice-givers crowd in on us whenever we have problems. Well-meaning friends and family members often seem to know exactly what we should do and how we should think. The Twelve-Step program cautions against giving advice, but even a nod or a sigh or an exclamation is often interpreted by us as advice when we are desperately searching for answers to problems. Such advice can add another layer of oppression to an already overwhelming situation. Sometimes we find ourselves acting on advice so we do not offend the advice-giver rather than because we feel it is good advice.

The writer of the Book of Proverbs says that knowing the Wisdom of God as reflected in Proverbs will help us sort out wisdom from foolishness and help us discern what is best for us. As receivers of advice, we need the Wisdom of God to help us make the very difficult choices that problems force on us.

May the Source of our being give us Wisdom to know what is best for our lives.

January 6

Those who know you, Lord, will trust you, for you do not abandon those who turn to you. PSALM 9:10

The Third Step in the Twelve-Step program for spiritual recovery calls for decision-making, perhaps the most important decision we will ever make. It is the decision to turn our will and our lives over to God. The psalmist tells us that God, like a mother with open arms, never abandons any of her children, never turns anyone away, never is unwilling to nourish anyone who comes searching for spiritual food.

For those whose lives have been filled with pain, injustice, and abuse, it is difficult to envision God as anything but an indifferent being or one who punishes. The Third Step is a leap of faith, a decision to trust God even if we do not know if God is trustworthy. Like a child jumping from a countertop into the arms of a loving parent, we must decide to jump. Often we have nothing to go on but the words of others who have taken the chance before us and found that God is trustworthy. God will catch us and hold us tenderly.

May we be given the courage to leap into the loving arms of God.

January 7

Do not abandon Wisdom, and she will protect you; love her, and she will keep you safe. PROVERBS 4:6

The Book of Proverbs presents the Wisdom of God as a woman, Sophia, who stands at the gates of the city calling out to all who pass by, "Listen to me." Her purpose is to tell us how to live so that we will be protected from behavior that is self-destructive. The assumption in her message is that we are responsible people, that we can make good choices. But, even more important is the underlying message that God is for us, that all of God's Wisdom is meant to make our lives more serene, more productive, more loving.

The writer of this verse tells us to love Wisdom. When we love someone, we want to know all there is to know about that person. We want to be close, to touch and be touched. We want to trust that person and believe that we will never be deserted. When we love, we live with hope for an ever-deepening relationship. Love Wisdom, and she will keep you safe.

May we hear the call of Wisdom and let her touch our lives.

January 8

It is dangerous to be concerned with what others think of you, but if you trust the Lord, you are safe.
PROVERBS 29:25

"But what will people think?" marches through our minds like a drumbeat, shortening our stride, keeping us from walking freely. It stops us from admitting to others our most difficult problems, our deepest fears. It prevents us from reaching out for help. It forces us to wear a mask that keeps others from ever really knowing us. Even though we want more than anything to be known, to be loved, to be accepted just as we are, still our fear of what others will think blocks us from being honest and open.

But, think for a moment about the persons we care for the most. Is it because they are perfect that we love them? Is it because they never have a problem that we respect them? We are pulled like a magnet to persons who are imperfect, human, vulnerable, struggling, and open. Yet, we assume that we will be rejected if we let others see those very things in ourselves. God accepts and loves us, knowing all there is to know. We need to trust that others will, also.

May God give us courage to be honest and open with others.

January 9

Lord, who may enter your Temple? . . . a person who obeys God in everything and always does what is right. PSALM 15:1-2

What an impossible demand. Who would ever be allowed into God's presence? And yet, the psalmist insists that our behavior has much to do with our relationship to God. God, who is love, wants us to have a loving relationship with ourselves and with others. The things we do that block that love also become barriers between us and God.

The Fourth Step is a fearless moral inventory. It is a time when we write down all those things about ourselves that are loving and helpful and all those things that are hurtful, that act like a dam preventing the free, rushing flow of love through our lives. The Fourth Step takes days, maybe weeks, of intense self-searching, peeling back layer after layer until we stand unprotected, bare, and human before ourselves and God. Fearsome as the task seems at the outset, the result is always relief. "I am both good and bad, strong and weak. I can accept that." And so does God!

May God give us the freedom that comes from facing ourselves honestly and openly.

January 10

The Lord is righteous and loves good deeds; those who do them will live in the Lord's presence. PSALMS 11:7

God delights in those things we do that promote our health and well-being and the well-being of others. And God wants *us* to feel good about them, also. A major part of the Fourth-Step inventory is discovering all those things about ourselves that are good. But we find that it is often easier to prepare a dirge of our failings than a litany of our strengths. It is often easier to cite occasions when we have fallen short than to recount the times we have done good things, things that were helpful both to self and to others. And it is even more difficult to talk to others about our strengths. We are afraid of seeming conceited or setting ourselves up for others to knock down.

As we become more and more used to thinking of ourselves as competent, responsible, caring people, we find ourselves standing tall with no need to boast, taking long strides with no thought of appearing proud. We enjoy and use the gifts God has given us, fully conscious of the giver and of our own value as God's children.

May God fill us with an awareness of all that is good in ourselves.

January 11

Teach a child how to live, and the child will remember it all through life. PROVERBS 22:6

Nearly three thousand years ago, the writer of this verse recognized what modern psychologists teach – that there is a direct link between what a child is taught through words and experiences and the way that person lives the rest of his or her life. We are all products of our childhoods.

However, we do not need to be victims of our childhoods. We remember either consciously or sub-consciously all that has happened to us. The good news is that, if those memories are hurtful, we do not need to let them destroy us. But diffusing this destructive power is not easy. In fact, it is probably one of the most difficult tasks we will ever attempt. And we can almost never accomplish it alone. But the release we can experience when we allow painful memories to surface – and then see them with new understanding – is well worth any effort. The process is like the lancing of a boil; it allows the poison to escape and the wound to heal.

May our Comforter help us find ways to heal the deep wounds from our childhoods.

January 12

I have seen everything done in this world, and I tell you, it is all useless. It is like chasing the wind.
ECCLESIASTES 1:14

We do not know where it comes from or where it goes, but we feel the wind. It pushes us and everyone around us in the same direction. The easiest thing to do is to go with the wind, to even chase after it.

That wind may be the desire for money or success, prestige or control. Our culture sweeps people along in the wind of pride and materialism, of competition and accomplishment. To go with the wind seems like the reasonable way, but when we look back on our lives, we will say with the writer of Ecclesiastes, "It was all useless."

To achieve what is truly useful, what is deeply meaningful, we need to turn and face the wind, feel it blow past us, struggle against its power. We must stop and look at ourselves, asking the question, "What gives me *real* satisfaction and lasting contentment?" Finding the answers may take years, but once we know them, our lives fall into perspective. Then the "wind" loses its power over us.

May God give us the courage and strength to face the wind.

January 13

There are people who think they are so good—oh, how good they think they are! PROVERBS 30:13

The writer of this verse reflects a common judgmental attitude people have toward others. The statement is often followed by, "But, do you know what I heard?" We delight in finding faults in others, especially those we think consider themselves to be better than we are. Often our delight is rooted in a need to justify our own behavior, to raise ourselves by lowering someone else.

Our assessment of the other may be correct. That person may be suffering from an acute case of self-righteousness. But, as we grow toward spiritual wholeness, we learn that it is not our business to judge another. We are only responsible for ourselves, for taking our own inventory.

We do this, not by measuring ourselves against someone else, but by establishing our own goals and then looking honestly at ways that we have moved toward those goals and ways that we have moved away from them. Our task is ourselves.

May God help us keep our eyes on our own goals.

January 14

Thoughtless words can wound as deeply as any sword. PROVERBS 12:18A

Children use the rhyme, "Sticks and stones may break my bones, but words can never hurt me," but even children know better. Words have an enormous power over the way we think and feel about ourselves and about others. As adults we are often living with unsutured wounds caused by thoughtless words of another – a parent, out of exasperation, cut us with sarcasm; a trusted friend gave us a tongue lashing. Verbal abuse can be as damaging as physical abuse, and our hurt can easily turn to resentment, anger, or – worst of all – self-hate.

We cannot control the words of others. Neither can we pretend those words were never spoken. But we can try to respond in ways that help us rather than hurt us. If our negative behavior has prompted the hurtful words, then we need to take a good look at our behavior and try to change. But if the words were simply a reflection of the other's own dis-ease, then they can be set aside. Responding with angry words or hostile silence only makes our own problems worse.

May God help us work toward healing the wounds caused by thoughtless or cruel words.

January 15

. . . but wisely spoken words can heal. PROVERBS 12:18B

Like fire that can warm a house and make it cozy or burn it to the ground, so words have the power to build up or destroy, to heal or to wound. We have all heard healing words, and we all have the capacity to speak them. It is exciting to know that our tongues have as much power to help another heal as do the healing ointments we apply to wounds.

Our responsibility as recovering people is to try to use our tongues wisely and compassionately. (Whether the other person "hears" or not is out of our hands.) Words that build up—such as "I love you," "I'm proud of you," "I'm with you"—can flow freely from our tongues when they truly come from our hearts.

Promise yourself that this day you will speak a healing word to each of the important persons in your life. In return, expect the satisfaction that comes from knowing you are using what power you have to help another.

May our Creator fill our hearts with love so that our words will heal.

January 16

I have learned why people work so hard to succeed; it is because they envy the things their neighbors have. But it is useless. It is like chasing the wind. ECCLESIASTES 4:4

Envy is considered one of the seven cardinal sins. Sin is that behavior which sets up barriers between ourselves and others and between ourselves and God. Certainly envy does that. Envying others means that we want what they have. It means that we are dissatisfied with ourselves, that we do not accept our lives. At some level we likely blame God for giving us such a sorry lot in life when others have so much. So we pray for more, and when God does not give us what we want, we assume there is no God or that God does not care about us.

There is also direct correlation between the amount of envy we allow into our lives and our inability to either love or understand others. If we envy a person because it appears that person has more than we—more money, more possessions, more power, more serenity, more love—we lose the ability to see beneath the surface of his or her life. Envy undercuts our efforts to be all that we are meant to be by blocking the flow of love into and out of us.

May our Deliverer release us from the power of envy.

January 17

Even before I speak, you already know what I will say. PSALM 139:4

The child was four when he threw a ball and broke a glass vase. His parents knew he had done it, but he insisted that it must have been the baby or the dog. For days they waited, watching as his relationship with them deteriorated. Then, one night, he came with tear-streaked face and said, "I did it. I broke the vase." They took him in their arms, dried his tears, and held him close.

The Fifth Step is a chance to tell God and one other person all of those things that have been eating away at our souls, diminishing our capacity to love and be loved. These might include our deliberate, hurtful actions. Often they encompass our reactions to times we have been hurt — angers we have justified, resentments we have fed.

God already knows all of this, just as parents often know long before they are told. But there is great power in the telling, in the confession, power that releases love so it can flow with abandon.

May the Source of life give us the courage to confess.

January 18

Two are better than one because together they can work more effectively. ECCLESIASTES 4:9

These words are deceptively simple, and it is easy to say, "Yes, of course, everyone knows that." And yet, there are many parts of our lives where we choose to go it alone. We cut others out and resist what we see as intrusion. Often these are the occasions where we most need another, where we can never get a true perspective by ourselves.

Many of us involved in a Twelve-Step program have discovered the indescribable value of a sponsor—one other person to whom we can turn with any and all problems, one who cares about us and is always looking out for our well-being. We have also discovered, most likely, the value of a group where people gather to share honestly and deeply, to support and help each other. In these groups people avoid advising or exerting control over another, but they give to each other what we all need most—affirmation, honesty, strength, and love. This enables us to see anew our own problems and then work to change those things we can change.

May our Helper bless us with companions for our journey.

January 19

Lord, I have so many enemies! PSALM 5:8A

Enemies can be found in many places, but the most frustrating enemy is the enemy within. It is that part of self that stubbornly resists change. It might be an inner voice telling us we are inadequate, incapable, or unloveable. Or, perhaps it is our inner voice whispering, "The real problem is not me, it's my partner or my job or my child." This enemy insists that the real problem is on the outside and that, until we can fix it, our lives will be miserable.

But the spiritual journey of the Twelve Steps has now led us to that point where we have recognized our powerlessness over much that is outside of ourselves, and we have turned our attention to what is within us instead. We have determined that we have hurt ourselves in many ways. We realize that many of our problems have been made worse by the ways we have handled them. Now we stand ready to have God remove all these shortcomings, these self-defeating attitudes, these unloving responses. We want to let go of these enemies, to change, to be made new. This is the Sixth Step toward spiritual recovery.

May the Source of our being give us freedom from our enemies within.

January 20

Lead me to do your will; make your way plain for me to follow. PSALM 5:8B

We have made ourselves ready through the first six Steps. Step Seven tells us to take action, to ask God to remove all our shortcomings. The assumption of this Step is that we cannot do it ourselves, any more than we can change other people ourselves. But we can ask God to change us. And God has promised to do just that. The change is not instantaneous. We do not attain perfection overnight. In fact, we never do. But now we can begin the life-long process of asking God to remove our shortcomings, one at a time, in God's time.

If holding grudges has been a pattern in our lives, a pattern that destroys loving relationships with others, then we can ask, daily, that God will break the pattern, releasing us from that destructive habit. And if we are truly ready to be free, if we really want to give up that response, God will take it away in time, freeing us to look openly at other areas of our lives.

May our Leader set us on a new path this day.

January 21

How long must I endure trouble? How long will sorrow fill my heart day and night? PSALM 13:2A

The psalmist cries out, pleading for an end to the trouble and sorrow that fill his heart. Often trouble and sorrow in our lives have their roots in broken relationships. Through the Fourth and Fifth Steps we came to realize our own culpability. It was not always the other person's fault. In fact, our behavior, our anger, our resentment, our thoughtlessness, our self-justification often hurt others. The original crack in the relationship may have been caused by the other, but our response produced the shattering. Or perhaps we are responsible for the original crack.

Step Eight tells us to set aside all questions of primary fault and make a list of the persons we have harmed and all relationships we have strained or shattered through our behavior or attitudes. When we take concrete steps to determine whom we have hurt and start making amends to those persons, some of our sorrow can begin to lift.

May God lift the sorrow from our hearts as we accept responsibility for the times we have hurt others.

January 22

People do all their work just to get something to eat, but they never have enough. ECCLESIASTES 6:7

In some places in the world, this is literally true. People work from morning till night and never earn enough money or grow enough food to feed themselves and their families. But for many of us who have more than we need and often eat more than we should, these words still ring true. There is an insatiability in the human spirit, an emptiness, a place that is never filled. No matter what we get or what we have, it is never enough. So, we keep searching, being disappointed in anything or anyone that does not fully satisfy us.

If our goal is to live in a constant state of satisfaction, we will always be frustrated, we will never have enough.

As we move toward spiritual recovery, one of the things that happens to us is that the insatiability, which used to send us off on a desperate quest for satisfaction, now speaks to us of our humanity. This emptiness, common to all, motivates us toward growth, not gluttony. It links us to others.

May the Creator of all give us a deep understanding of our oneness with others.

January 23

Some friendships do not last, but some friends are more loyal than brothers or sisters. PROVERBS 18:24

Make a mental list of all of the persons in your life that you have called "friend." Even if you eliminate all those persons who you realize in retrospect were not really friends, all those who were not concerned about you or your well-being, the list very likely still contains at least a few names.

We allow others to touch our lives and to become friends for a variety of reasons. Most often the reason has to do with our own need. Some friends are persons to have fun with; others are persons we can talk with about problems. Some friends are strong themselves, carrying us through rough waters; other friends give *us* the chance to be strong. We may even be blessed with one or two life-long friends. These friends are flexible, resilient, and loving enough to accept all our changes, all our growth, and to find common ground no matter where we stand.

All through our lives, God works through our friends to meet our needs, to touch us in deep and meaningful ways.

May God bless us with good friends.

January 24

God remembers those who suffer; God does not forget their cry. PSALM 9:12A

Step Nine sets us loose in our world to make amends to all those whom we have hurt. It is a very important part of our own spiritual journey, but it also enables us to be God's hands on earth. God loves those persons whom we have hurt. God has not forgotten their pain. And now God can use us to help in the healing of others.

The important and very tricky part of this Step is to always have the well-being of the other as our top priority. Confession, for instance, might be good for our souls, but it could deeply hurt the person to whom we are confessing. If our direct attempt to relieve our own guilt and make amends could increase the suffering of the other, then we need to find an indirect way, a more compassionate way. The Ninth Step asks us to try to think as God thinks, to love as God loves. It asks us to make amends for our own wrongs in ways that wipe away the tears and build up the other person.

May God inspire us to find healing ways to make amends.

January 25

I praise the Lord because he guides me, and in the night my conscience warns me. PSALM 16:7

Our spiritual journey has brought us to the place where, by taking a personal inventory, we daily face who we are. When we are wrong, we admit it both to ourselves and to the persons we have wronged. We also rejoice when we have made good choices. The process we experienced in Steps Four through Nine now becomes a part of the way we habitually think. We rely on God to guide us and we rely on our conscience to warn us if we are slipping back into old habits, into destructive ways of living that work against us.

Practicing the Tenth Step helps us experience the wonderful gift of the simple words, "I'm sorry." When these words are spoken from the depths of our hearts with no intent to manipulate the other and with every intent to change our behavior, they heal relationships. Unlike a band-aid that covers a wound, they work as a healing balm, penetrating the bruise, cleaning it, preventing infection. Wrongs we do not admit to ourselves remain as sores on our spirits. Wrongs we cannot confess infect our relationships.

May the words "I'm sorry" flow freely from our hearts.

January 26

The best thing a person can do is eat, drink, and enjoy what he or she has earned. And yet, I realized that even this comes from God. ECCLESIASTES 2:24

There is a very fine line between the philosophy of some to "eat, drink, and be merry," and one of the primary concepts of the Twelve-Step program, which is to live one day at a time. It is the difference between irresponsible living and responsible living, the difference between living for the moment because we have no regard for the future and living for the moment in order to keep fear of the future from immobilizing us. It is the difference between indulging in pleasure for its own sake and trying to recognize what is good in each day in order to treasure it.

It is also the difference between blotting out the past through over-indulgence and choosing to live free of old hurts, guilts, and resentments. It is the difference between pretending the past does not exist and choosing to lighten our load by keeping our focus on the day.

Living one day at a time enables us to open each day as a gift from the Source of all good gifts and treasure it to the fullest.

May the Source of life give us joy and peace this day.

January 27

Look at me, O Lord my God, and answer me. Restore my strength; don't let me die. PSALM 13:3

The Eleventh Step brings us full circle. In Step One we admitted our powerlessness over much in our lives. The subsequent Steps move us through the painstaking and often painful process of turning our eyes inward, examining ourselves, and then beginning the restoration of our relationships with God and with others. And now, in the Eleventh Step, we are again talking about power, praying for power, or, as the psalmist puts it, asking God to restore our strength.

We are not left powerless for our life's journey, but the power is not just our own. There is an energy supply available from the Source of all energy. One way to tap into it is through prayer and meditation. With the psalmist we plead with God to look at us and not let us die. We ask God to give us the energy and the power we need to continue our life's journey.

May God look at us today and answer our prayers for power.

January 28

God sets a time for birth and a time for death. ECCLESIASTES 3:2A

"For everything there is a season . . . ," the writer of Ecclesiastes tells us. Birth and death are the inevitable beginning and end of us all. But between our physical birth and the death of our bodies, we experience any number of births and deaths. Some people talk about being given new life or being transformed as a way of describing a point of major change in their lives.

All spiritual renewal involves the death of old habits, old priorities, old ways of relating to others, and the birth of something new. This might be the death of always wanting accompanied by the birth of joy in giving or the death of resentment coupled with the birth of tolerance. It could be the death of cynicism and the birth of hope. Or it might be the death of self-hate and the birth of self-acceptance. It often involves the death of doubt and anger toward God and the birth of a trusting relationship, beginning tentatively, but growing as God proves trustworthy.

May God create a new birth in our lives.

January 29

They are like trees that grow beside a stream, that bear fruit at the right time, and whose leaves do not dry up. PSALM 1:3

The psalmist might well have been talking about those who carry the message of spiritual recovery to others and practice it in all their affairs. "They are like trees that grow beside a stream." Their roots have tapped into an unending source of life-giving water, God's love and strength. These persons also bear fruit at the right time. In other words, they have a sixth sense about the needs of others. When the time is right, their words, their love, their actions can bring to others the message of the possibility for spiritual recovery and renewal.

In our own spiritual journey, when we have admitted our powerlessness over others, we can bring the message without coercion or manipulation and without having our egos involved in their response. The lives of those we touch are in God's hands just as our lives are. Our responsibility is only to allow ourselves to be nourished so that we can bear fruit. This is the Twelfth Step.

May our Creator help us grow strong and bear much fruit.

January 30

Correct someone, and afterward that person will appreciate it more than flattery. PROVERBS 28:23

How can we reconcile the advice to correct others with the principle of not judging, of not taking another's inventory? What is our responsibility when we hear or see others doing something to themselves, or thinking in some way, that runs counter to the principles we are learning through the Scripture and the Twelve Steps?

Our first task is to be sure that our primary concern is for the other and not for self-aggrandizement. Then we must always realize that our analysis could be wrong, our judgment faulty. And our perspective always needs to be colored by the belief that the person is in God's hands. It is not our responsibility to fix anyone.

Finally, our correction should always be gentle guidance, not dogmatic judgment, reflecting the principles we have learned, the wisdom we have gained. It is possible to find a way to keep our focus on our own inventory and also accept the positive role we can play in the lives of others.

May God give us wisdom and kindness as we live in relationships with others.

January 31

If you oppress poor people, you insult the God who made them; but kindness shown to the poor is an act of worship. PROVERBS 14:31

What does it mean to be poor? The writer of this verse was probably thinking of those who have no money, who perhaps are homeless or destitute. But poverty has many forms. Some people are poor because they live without love. Others are poor because they lack hope. Still others live with the poverty that comes from disillusionment, from being let down by those they trusted.

It takes compassionate eyes to want to see those living in obvious poverty. It takes *perceptive* eyes to see the poverty in lives that appear affluent.

But seeing is not enough. We are called to show kindness, to do something. But we live with the reality that sometimes what we think of as kindness does not always work for the other's well-being. Because we are not told exactly what to do, our challenge is to see poverty where it exists and respond creatively to the individual needs of the other person.

May the Source of our being make us perceptive and willing to act.

february

February 1

What are people, that you think of them; mere humans, that you care for them? PSALM 8:4

This question follows three verses praising the maker of the moon and the stars. How could a God who set in motion the universe, who is the guiding force behind all of creation, care about me – one person out of billions? What arrogance to think that the Creator of all is concerned about my hurt and pain and guilt! What ego to assume that God is working in my life to give me wholeness and health! What pride to think that the Source of all life could use me to bring healing and hope to another.

And yet, this is the kind of God we have – a God who never turns away. Our God cradles us like a mother and then sets us down to test our own legs, patiently picking us up when we fall, kissing away the hurt, and giving us the courage to walk again. Our Creator is deeply concerned about our relationships with others, concerned enough to give us thousands of words of Wisdom for living in relationships.

To the question, "What am I that you care for me?" God answers, "You are my creation, made in my image."

May our Creator fill us with a sense of our glory.

February 2

It is useless, useless. . . . Life is useless, all useless.
ECCLESIASTES 1:2

Deep in the throes of a problem, surrounded by troubles, overwhelmed by concerns, it is easy to echo the words of the writer of Ecclesiastes, "Life is useless." We feel as if everything we do fails, everything we touch turns to dust.

Then we look around us and see others living good, happy lives, others no more deserving than we. And deep within us a voice cries out, "Nothing is fair!" We struggle to find a reason to go on living. We fight the temptation to give up.

For many the path to spiritual recovery begins here. Every other path we have tried has been a dead-end. We finally admit our helplessness. And so we turn to God and to others who have been where we are, to others who have felt the same desperate loneliness and deep frustration we feel. The Twelve Steps to spiritual recovery is one way to approach God, one way to reach for a new life. Others have found new wisdom through these Steps. Their experiences can keep us going and give us hope.

May God give us new meaning and hope for our lives.

February 3

Why are you so far away, O Lord? Why do you hide yourself when we are in trouble? PSALM 10:1

The greatest challenge to faith is the silence of God. Which one of us has not gone through such times? When we have hoped and prayed and struggled with a problem for years, we want to scream at God, "Look at me! See my trouble! Hear my cry! Do something!" But God seems so removed that we feel it is wasted effort.

This was the struggle of Job, a righteous man who lost everything in life that he valued, including his health. He railed at God, protesting his innocence, demanding an explanation for the misery of his life. His friends came and told him it must be his fault, something he had done. But Job knew he was blameless. Nothing he had ever done could possibly warrant such punishment. And God remained silent.

Sometimes, like Job, we eventually have the satisfaction of seeing in retrospect how all our troubles have worked together for good. But in the midst of the struggle, all we can do is try to remain faithful to a God who seems far away.

May our Comforter hear our cries and give us courage.

February 4

The Lord hears my weeping; God listens to my cry for help and will answer my prayer. PSALM 6:9

This statement of faith in a God who *is* listening, who *does* care, is at the root of the Second Step, "We come to believe. . . ." Our belief does not happen overnight or through an act of will. But it can begin to happen when we open ourselves to the possibility of a caring God, a power beyond ourselves that does, indeed, want our lives to be made whole and healthy.

The importance of this Step can hardly be overstated. Persons who spend their lives in bitterness and anger, overwhelmed and overcome by the reality of living in an imperfect world, are often persons who have never allowed themselves to receive the blessings and power of God. They have tried to by-pass that crucial process of coming to believe that a power greater than themselves does care and can help them restore their inner health. "Coming to believe" is a process we commit ourselves to initially in our journey, and then affirm daily.

May we come to believe that God wants to make us whole.

February 5

God sets a time for planting and a time for pulling up that which is planted. ECCLESIASTES 3:2B

Those of us who garden know that, if we plant too soon, we risk losing our investment. If we wait too long, the heat of the summer will scorch young plants or a fall freeze will prematurely kill them. Pulling up what has been planted must also be done at the right time.

God's gracious timing also guides our lives. We experience times when ideas and habits are planted and nurtured and times when they are pruned or pulled up. There are times when new relationships are planted and times when they are severed. There are times when faith is planted and times when faith is uprooted and doubt takes over. Only then can stronger faith blossom. Our lives fall into seasons almost as predictable as the seasons of the year. We are never too old for new seeds to be planted and never too young for what has grown in us to be pruned or pulled up. And in both the planting and the pulling up, God's love and graciousness are evident.

May we recognize God's timing in our lives.

February 6

If it is cold, two can sleep together and stay warm, but how can you keep warm by yourself? ECCLESIASTES 4:11

A rule of survival if you and another are caught outdoors in a cold winter storm is to take off your clothing and cuddle as close as you can, wrapping the clothes around both of you. Flesh next to flesh maintains heat longer.

Our emotional lives are like that, also. In the midst of the worst storms, our chances for survival are much greater if we "take off our clothes," if we draw close to someone, allowing ourselves to be vulnerable, baring our souls, soaking up the warmth of the other.

Often people have to seek professionals in order to find that safe place where they can expose their deepest feelings. But that can also be the function of friends, of the group. With such friends, persons trying to survive a storm can find warmth, comfort, and help.

The real joy of giving warmth to another is that we, also, can be vulnerable, can lay open our hearts and receive warmth in return.

May our Refuge make us a safe place for others.

February 7

The Lord reached down from above and took hold of me, pulling me out of the deep waters. PSALM 18:16

The Second Step describes coming to a point of belief in a power greater than ourselves. Many people reach this stage and then wonder why they do not experience God's actions in their lives. The next Step pushes us into deep and often scary water. It is capsulated in the slogan, "Let Go and Let God." It forces us beyond the point of saying, "Yes, I believe that God's loving arms are around me," to the point of falling back into those arms.

We can spend our whole lives believing. But if we never trust that belief by surrendering our will, we will be locked into a life of frustration and impotence. We will try desperately to pull ourselves together, fix the problems in our lives, and make it on our own. The Third Step asks us to turn our will and lives over to the care of God. Only then will God have the chance to reach out with loving hands and pull us out of the deep waters.

May God give us the courage to let go and let God take hold of us.

February 8

Gossip is spread by wicked people; they stir up trouble and break up friendships. PROVERBS 16:28

The writer spares no words in denouncing those who spread gossip. But who of us can say we have never fallen into that trap? Gossip is so interesting to listen to, and once known, it screams to be told.

The writer calls the spreaders of gossip "wicked" and then goes on to tell why they deserve that judgment: they stir up trouble and break up friendships. There is something sacred about the bonds between persons. It is as if God is in the connection, or that God *is* the connection. Anything that severs that connection is wrong. Gossip, clearly, can stretch and break the bonds between people, and so those who engage in it are called wicked. Or, more accurately, the action is wicked.

To help ourselves avoid such action, it is best to avoid those people or situations where we would likely hear gossip. But, if we do hear it, we need to ask for the power of God to keep us from stirring up trouble and help us to preserve friendships.

May our Deliverer keep us from the destructive power of gossip.

February 9

I say to the Lord, "You are my Lord; all the good things I have come from you." PSALM 16:2

As our spirituality deepens, we move from blaming God for all our troubles to thanking God for all our blessings. But before we can do that, we need to have clear vision to look within and around us and see what is good. It is as if we have had dark lenses taped to our eyes and we have to rip them off, give our eyes time to adjust to the light, and then start looking.

As we look within, we discover that our strengths may include a strong will to survive, a willingness to reach out for help, honesty about our feelings, openness to the needs of others, deep loyalty, cheerfulness, patience with some of the people in our lives, or courage to face difficult situations.

While doing the Fourth Step, we need to determine what our failings are, but it is equally important to discover our strengths and to glory in them. They are gifts from the Source of all life, who wants us to enjoy them.

May the Source of our lives help us see all that is good about us.

February 10

Look at what happens in the world; sometimes righteous people get the punishment of the wicked, and wicked people get the reward of the righteous.
ECCLESIASTES 8:14

It is hard to deny this statement. But think about the attitude behind such a statement. It is based on the assumption that we can and should make judgments about who is righteous and who is wicked or that people of the world can be divided into two groups, the good and the bad. It is also based on the assumption that certain things are always rewards and other things are always punishments.

Those of us wanting to grow spiritually need to guard against making judgments about others. Nothing is as it appears. We are not in a position to decide who is worthy and who is not. And we also cannot know what is a reward and what is not. Money, for instance, can be a curse or a blessing to those living with it. Nothing is as it appears to the outsider. Our belief in a Highest Power that is both merciful and just allows us to live and let live, leaving both judgment and consequence to God.

May God guard us from a spirit of judgment.

February 11

But in the traps they set for others, they themselves get caught. PSALM 7:15

There is a certain inevitability expressed in this verse. If we "set a trap" for another, it will, instead, trap us. These traps have many forms, but at the heart of them all there is an attempt to control, manipulate, trick, or use another.

The trap might be an attempt to manipulate a friend or partner into giving us a compliment, or to set up our children to feel sorry for us. We might attempt to trick another into an admission of guilt or lure him or her into asking our advice. The trap might be an attempt to use a friend for our own purposes.

Whenever we set a trap for another, we open the door for our own entrapment. This cycle in one form or another repeats itself over and over again until we learn to accept others as they are and work only on our own improvement, our own journey. When we live freely, we not only show love and respect for others by not setting traps for them, but we can also live more fully because there is no risk that we wil be caught in our own traps.

May God keep us from trapping and entrapment.

February 12

You know my heart. You have come to me at night; you have examined me completely. PSALM 17:3

The psalmist describes a passive process where, without our help, God sees into our hearts and knows us.

The Fifth Step involves an active process, a way of saying, "Yes, God, I, too, have examined my heart, and I am willing to admit to you the exact nature of my wrongs."

But it is not enough to confess to God. Our wrongs have all been played out in the arena of life. Nothing we are or do is without social consequence. And, so, in the Fifth Step we acknowledge the reality of this life in relationship by having another person present, a person who represents all others. Before that person we admit all we have done to hurt others and to hurt ourselves. And from that person we receive acceptance and forgiveness. He or she ushers us into a new way of relating to others based on trust, honesty, and vulnerability. Through the Fifth Step, we can begin to accept ourselves because we know that both God and another person know us and accept us just as we are.

May the Creator of all give us the peace that comes from being known fully and accepted.

February 13

Peace of mind makes the body healthy, but jealousy is like a cancer. PROVERBS 14:30

Cancer begins with a single cell that becomes abnormal and begins reproducing itself, forming masses that cut off the normal functioning of our organs. Jealousy is like that. It begins with a single wish—perhaps to be better or have more than another—and then grows, forming masses of resentment and envy, affecting our spiritual lives, choking off love and trust. And, because we are whole beings, what affects our spirits, affects our minds and bodies.

By contrast, the writer points out that peace of mind makes the body healthy. The gift of serenity, which we all desire, is a gift that will affect our whole being.

The teenager's hacking cough had gone on for many months. Nothing doctors recommended helped. Then someone suggested perhaps the problem was in the spirit. He should write down everything from the past year about which he felt guilty, and, when the list was complete, ask God for forgiveness and then burn it. He did as he was told, and within days the cough was gone.

May God give us peace of mind and body.

February 14

The Lord helped me out of danger; God saved me because God was pleased with me. PSALM 18:19

When we finally realize the extent of our wrongdoing through our Fifth Step, it is hard to believe that God could be pleased with us. But it gives God pleasure when we come to God as to a loving parent and admit our faults.

With this new knowledge of self and God, we are ready for the Sixth Step: to have God remove these defects of character. The difficulty with this Step is the deep ambivalence we have toward letting go of certain character traits, even if they are destructive. They are like old glasses. They may be bad for our eyes, but they are comfortable, and change requires a period of discomfort. For instance, a certain satisfaction in self-righteousness may be hard to give up. Or there may be a wonderful built-in defense in thinking less of ourselves than we should. If we see ourselves as victims, we never have to take responsibility for our own lives. Change is scary. Old habits die hard. But we need to be ready to have God change us in order to continue our spiritual recovery.

May our Helper give us the deep desire to change, to be made new.

February 15

The helpless commit themselves to you; you have always helped the needy. PSALM 10:14

A certain paradox exists in this verse and in the Seventh Step. "Committing ourselves to God," or, as the Seventh Step puts it, "Asking God to remove our shortcomings," is an action that takes great strength, great courage. In one sense, we are helpless, needy, humble – we have squarely faced our weaknesses. But, in a much more profound sense, we have tapped into the power we have. This is the power to take responsibility for our own lives and say, "I am not going to live this way anymore. I am going to change all the things I can change. I am going to move from frustrating attempts at self-change to fervently asking God to change me."

We cannot take hate from our hearts, but God can. We cannot just stop resenting or judging or blaming or hurting ourselves or others, but God can help us stop. All we need to do is ask daily, hourly, and God will begin the process of nudging us out of old habits, thoughts, and actions, and begin creating in us a new and healthier self.

May we experience the wonder of God's re-creative power in our lives.

February 16

Hate stirs up trouble, but love forgives all offenses.
PROVERBS 10:12

All offenses? That is a pretty heavy order. Surely there must be some middle ground between being the hateful stirrer up of trouble and being one who forgives *all* offenses. Couldn't we just forgive those things which we are asked to forgive? Wouldn't it be all right to tolerate persons we cannot forgive, just so long as we don't hate them?

But the writer allows for no middle ground, recognizing that if someone has enough influence in our lives to hurt us, not forgiving that action will inevitably discolor our relationship. We open the door to hate – "and hate stirs up trouble" – increasing animosity between us and the other person and producing spiritual poison within ourselves.

The antidote is forgiveness. Love not only requires that we forgive, but it also enables us to forgive – even before we are asked. Forgiveness is, ultimately, the way we show greatest love for ourselves because it frees us from the burdens of hate, anger, and resentment.

May God fill our hearts with love and forgiveness.

February 17

Wisdom is more valuable than jewels; nothing you could want can compare with it. PROVERBS 3:15

God appears to King Solomon in a dream and asks Solomon what he wants. Instead of asking for riches or power or a long life, Solomon asks for wisdom. God, very pleased with his request, gives him not only wisdom but riches and power besides.

Wisdom is more than knowledge, more than reason, more than scientific data, although those things may contribute to wisdom. Wisdom begins with a relationship to God. It flows out of our spirits and then through our minds. The most knowledgeable people on earth have made and continue to make serious, costly mistakes. Wisdom leads a person to know instinctively which paths to follow, which doors to open. Wise people are often recognized by others, but they never claim the wisdom as their own. They live in humility and trust, fully aware of the limits of their knowledge and the fallibility of their reason. A wise person gives top priority to his or her spiritual growth, and this perspective illuminates the rest of life.

May God give us the desire for wisdom.

February 18

Turn away from evil and do good; strive for peace with all your heart. PSALM 34:14

Between the two phrases of this verse, there is an implied question, "How?" "How can I turn away from evil and do good?" and the answer has three key words, *strive, peace,* and *heart.*

We must *strive.* There is action involved, effort expected, energy needed. A part of this process of striving is embodied in the Eighth Step. As we make a list of all the persons we have hurt, we need to envision each person with love and pray for a willingness to make amends.

Peace establishes the goal—inner peace and peace in our relationships. This goal of peace, serenity, contentment, replaces other goals, goals such as perfection, justice, happiness, or success.

Turning from evil and doing good are overt actions. But they begin in our *hearts.* Good actions spring from a good heart, so our primary task is to continually ask God to create in us a pure heart.

May the Source of life energize us as we strive for peace in all our relationships.

February 19

Tears may flow in the night, but joy comes in the morning. PSALM 30:5B

She wept in her friend's arms that night as she poured out her guilt for having broken her friend's trust—broken trust through a broken confidence. She made no attempt to justify her behavior, no attempt to share the blame. She said simply, "I've failed you and hurt you. Can you forgive me?" Then they both wept tears of lost innocence.

The night passed, and with the morning came a deep joy. A relationship that had been broken was now healing.

The Ninth Step asks us to take each name on our list of persons we have hurt and carefully decide how best we can make amends to that person. Sometimes those amends involve confession and forgiveness. Sometimes the most loving thing to do is to keep our hurtful actions to ourselves and try in any way we can to live responsible, loving lives toward those persons. Sometimes it involves restitution of property. Amends can take many forms, but, if done with love and prayer, they work toward healing.

May our Comforter and Healer give us joy in the morning.

February 20

Better to eat vegetables with people you love than to eat the finest meat where there is hate. PROVERBS 15:17

She walked into the lovely home and could immediately feel the tension. Hors d'oeuvres were served, but the hostess's hand trembled as she set the plate down. The guests tried to make light conversation, but the silence that followed a sharp exchange between host and hostess was difficult to fill. As the evening progressed, the delicious food began to leave a bitter after-taste.

The writer of this proverb tells us that it is better to eat less in an atmosphere of love than to eat well in a place where all one feels is tension. Doctors would agree, stressing the importance of calm dining. But what do we do if our meal times, whether at home or away, are filled with tension? It gives us a good opportunity to practice the serenity prayer—accepting gracefully and calmly what we cannot change (others in the room); changing what we can (our own response); and knowing the difference. It is possible to remain calm in the midst of a stressful situation—not easy, but possible.

May God help us calmly accept what we cannot change.

February 21

Teach me your ways, O Lord; make them known to me. PSALM 25:4

We need to be taught the ways of God because they so often run counter to our ways. We want to acquire, God wants us to give. We try to get even, God tells us to forgive. We put self first, God tells us God is first. We strive for success, God emphasizes service.

As we spend our lives working on the Tenth Step – a daily personal inventory – we can look to God's wisdom as a guide. The exciting thing about this guide is that there is always new ground to cover, new territory to explore. We are never expected to reach perfection, only to keep traveling, keep learning, keep measuring our attitudes and behavior against God's standard.

Whenever we see ways in which we have failed, the Tenth Step tells us to promptly admit it. Gone are the days of self-justification and self-righteousness. We live, not in constant introspection, but with the freedom that comes from keeping our own slate clean.

May God continue to teach us new ways to live whole and healthy lives.

February 22

If you are lazy, you will never get what you are after.
PROVERBS 12:27A

The writer of this verse had in mind those who do not work very hard to earn a living. But, the verse can apply equally well to those of us who are seeking spiritual gifts. While these are all gifts from God, still, effort on our part is required to be ready to receive them.

It takes energy to break old, destructive thought patterns. It takes persistence to remember the new ways of thinking. And great discipline is required to maintain habits of meditation or regular meetings or talks with our sponsor or a good friend. It is frustrating how quickly those of us who are controllers fall back into that role again, or those of us who are passive slip back into being everyone's doormat. Those of us who were used to blaming the rest of the world for our troubles have to work hard to keep the focus on ourselves. And, if we struggle with pride, how easy it is to take credit when things go well.

God is waiting to do God's part. The rest is up to us.

May our Highest Power bless us with energy and discipline for our spiritual journeys.

February 23

Never ask, "Oh, why were things so much better in the old days?" It's not an intelligent question. ECCLESIASTES 7:10

Why is this not an intelligent question? Perhaps because our recollections of the past are never complete or even accurate. It is also not a helpful question because it keeps our focus on the past, making us dissatisfied and restless with the present.

It is impossible for us to dwell on the past (either the good or the bad) and, at the same time, live for today. All spiritual recovery is grounded in the present. We need to drop our focus on the past and our fears for the future, keeping our eyes on today—living it to the fullest.

For those of us who find ourselves glancing backward or forward, it sometimes helps to remember one of the Twelve-Step slogans such as "Let Go and Let God," "One day at a time," or "First things first." Repeating such a slogan to ourselves over and over until we really begin to act on it helps us keep our eyes on the present. It helps us ask the intelligent and helpful question, "How can I best live today?"

May God give us eyes that treasure the sights of each day.

February 24

But you, O God, are always my shield from danger; you give me victory and restore my courage. PSALM 3:3

The metaphor of life as an ongoing battle runs through this verse. We cannot escape the trials and tribulations common to all humanity. Sooner or later we all experience pain, brokenness, and grief. We must face the death of our dreams and the loss of our strength. Sometimes we feel as if we are being attacked from every side.

The Eleventh Step tells us to "seek through prayer and meditation to improve our conscious contact with God. . . ." God has promised to be like a shield for us in the battle, meeting the blows, preserving our lives. Through prayer and meditation we can call on God for help, and we can receive that help. We are not plucked from the battle, nor, in an instant, is truce declared and peace restored. The battle will still rage, the blows will still hurt, but our lives will be spared, our spirits strengthened, and our courage renewed.

May God be for us a protective shield in our battles.

February 25

In spite of all our work, there is nothing we can take with us. It isn't right! We go just as we came. ECCLESIASTES 5:15B–16

There is a real sense of futility in these verses, as if the writer saw no point in doing anything unless somehow that effort would be rewarded in an afterlife. It is the kind of orientation that measures everything by its future value: "Will this benefit me years from now?" "Will this help me succeed?" "Will I be rewarded for this effort sometime?"

By keeping our focus on one day at a time, we will be able to change this counterproductive way of thinking that often leads to futility. We will learn to rejoice in the *effort,* not the reward. Our eyes will focus on the goodness of the day – the loving interchange, the small, thoughtful gesture, the beauty of nature, the satisfaction of a job well done, the challenge of a difficult problem. By taking each day as it comes, we do not carry problems from the past or borrow problems from the future. Nor do we taint the efforts of the day by wondering if there will be a reward, if we will get our due. The day is sufficient in itself.

May the Creator of all bless and keep us this day.

February 26

I will praise you, Lord, with all my heart; I will tell of all the wonderful things you have done. PSALM 9:1

In his first devotional book, Oswald Chambers writes, "Spiritually, we cannot measure our lives by success, but only by what God pours through us, and we cannot measure that at all." The Twelfth Step has to do with what God pours through us to others. It has to do with "carrying the message to others," or "telling of all the wonderful things [God] has done."

Having had a spiritual awakening, we become like a conduit, channeling the love and power of God to others. Sometimes we "tell" through words, sometimes through actions. Sometimes the telling is conscious and premeditated, often it is unconscious and spontaneous. It is simply the living out of who we are.

Others cannot help but be touched by the genuine, nonmanipulative love and concern that flows from us. If they respond with openness and ask for help, we can direct them toward a path of spiritual recovery.

May God's love pour through us to others.

February 27

Trust in the Lord with all your heart. Never rely on what you think you know. PROVERBS 3:5

Rather than making us more and more sure of ourselves, age, experience, and honesty usually make us less sure of our knowledge, less secure in our decisions. Our experiences have taught us that our vision is always limited, and our judgments are always made on the basis of incomplete information. We know what it feels like to have been absolutely sure of something or someone and then be proved wrong.

The writer of Proverbs tells us to never rely on what we think we know. That does not mean we should live ineffective, indecisive, passive lives. What it means is that we act not out of arrogance but out of humility, knowing we could be wrong or partly wrong, but trusting that God can use even our mistakes for God's glory. There is a graciousness and freedom in such a life. We accept our fallibility, we admit our limits, and we trust God to use our lives and our mistakes in ways we can never know.

May our lives reflect God's glory.

February 28

Children, do what your father tells you and never forget what your mother taught you. Keep their words with you always, locked in your heart. PROVERBS 6:20–21

What an awesome responsibility this places on those of us who are parents or who have direct influence over young lives. Children may not always do what their parents or superiors tell them, but they never forget what they are taught. Those words are locked in their hearts.

What if those words are filled with put-downs: "How could you be so stupid?" "You're never going to get anywhere in life!" How will children feel about themselves with words such as these locked in their hearts? What will they have to go through to replace these destructive messages with good words, words that build them up?

The writer of Proverbs assumes that parents are wise, caring, and loving. As persons who affect young lives, we need to be continually working to live up to that image so that our children will be blessed and strengthened for their journeys by our words that are locked in their hearts.

May God fill us with wisdom and love as we influence young lives around us.

February 29

You spend your life working, laboring, and what do you have to show for it? ECCLESIASTES 1:3

Parents of teenagers often ask this question. After years of diaper changing, feeding, reading to, encouraging, praying for, and loving, they wake up one morning and find they are living with a hostile, moody, ungrateful child who seems to care little for them and not at all about their sacrifice.

But parents are not the only people who are angered by the disparity between effort and outcome. Who of us working for social change has not wondered if anything will ever really change or if all our efforts are little more than running on a treadmill.

Those of us who believe that the world is in the loving hands of God need never feel such despair. We know that we are required only to live as responsibly as we can. We are told only to keep walking, keep growing, keep doing what we are able to do. The results of our efforts are not in our hands. We do not need to measure success or failure or even progress. We need only live each day to our potential.

May our Deliverer free us from feelings of despair and failure.

march

March 1

Two are better than one . . . because if one falls, the other can help him or her up. But, if someone is alone and falls, it's just too bad, because there is no one to help. ECCLESIASTES 4:10

There are times when we can stumble and fall, pick ourselves up, and go on with our lives. But, there are some falls that leave us unable to rise by ourselves. At those times, it is important to have someone close, someone to reach down and help us up.

Still, it is sad to think that the only reason we seek companions on our life's journey is to have them around when we need them. A companion—someone with whom we can laugh or cry, in whom we can confide, and from whom we can receive love and affirmation—is good to have anytime.

Perhaps we can think of the easy times in life as those times when we have the energy to cultivate close friendships, to be for others what we would hope they would be for us during our difficult times. To have a friend, we must first be a friend.

May God make of us good friends to others.

March 2

When I lie down, I go to sleep in peace; you alone, O Lord, keep me perfectly safe. PSALM 4:8

It seemed as if it had been years since she had had a good night's sleep. The quiet set her mind free to dwell on one family crisis after another – a husband who drank too much, teenagers heavily involved in drug use. And when sleep came, terrifying nightmares took over, dreams of being crushed or chased or abused. Whether awake or asleep, she felt no serenity, no peace.

She read this verse, and it laid another burden on her: "If God really loved me, I could sleep in peace. Why doesn't God keep me safe?" And her turmoil increased.

Months went by, months of family tension and disintegration, until finally she knew she had to make hard choices. Somehow, she was given the strength to make them – and stick to them. She felt herself carried through a reality that exceeded her worst fears. Though forced to redefine "family" in her life, she found herself upheld and cared for in unexpected ways.

One day she awoke and realized that she had slept all night. God had kept her safe.

May our Comforter give us the precious gift of peaceful sleep.

March 3

I am worn out with grief; every night my bed is damp from weeping; my pillow is soaked with tears. PSALM 6:6

Grief, that deep, painful response to loss, comes to us at many points in our lives. Some of those losses are necessary and usually inevitable—movement out of our parental home, the death of parents or friends, the empty nest.

Other losses we bring upon ourselves by our own attitudes and behavior. We try to manage someone's life, and we find it all backfires on us. We set up false goals and false gods, and they crumble when we reach them. We carry within us a set of expectations for ourselves and others, and no one measures up. And so we grieve the death of dreams and the loss of power. Our lives have become unmanageable. The psalmist says, "I am worn out with grief. . . ." I am cold and alone.

At this point, we ask ourselves the questions, "Do I want my life to be different? Is there a way out when I feel as if I've tried everything? Am I ready to begin the long process of healing?" We are at the First Step toward spiritual recovery.

May the Source of life dry our tears and give us hope.

March 4

Generations come and generations go, but the world remains the same forever. ECCLESIASTES 1:4

Is this supposed to be good news or bad news? If it means that things are not getting any worse, then perhaps it is good news. But what about the implication that things cannot get any better? Is nothing we do going to have any lasting positive effect? Have we no control? No power? Why do we try? Are all our efforts futile?

The "burn-out" rate among those of us who take on the responsibility of fixing not only ourselves but also the world is 100 percent. Very quickly we feel as if we are trying to empty a swamp with a teacup.

The good news embedded in this statement is that our goal is not to change the world. Our goal is to live in the world as responsibly and lovingly as we can and to keep ourselves open to growth, maturity, and an ever-deepening spirituality. Our lives so lived will influence the world around us in positive ways, but we do not need to measure that influence, or even see it. Our lives *and* our world are in God's gracious hands.

May we be aware of God's presence in the world.

March 5

But I am no longer a person; I am a worm, despised and scorned by everyone. PSALM 22:6

The first thing the man did after plowing up a garden plot was to go and buy a large can of worms and "plant" them in the ground. The worms, simply by being what they are, made the soil more fertile and receptive to the seeds.

But the psalmist uses the image of worms to convey something quite different from this—the lowest possible feelings about self. And he implies that these feelings are caused or made worse by the attitudes of others. When we are despised by others we begin despising ourselves.

Many of us go through times in life when we are, in fact, looked down on by much of society. These times might be brought on by our addictions or the addiction of a family member. Divorce, poverty, illness, or other circumstances often beyond our control plummet us into despair. We feel useless, unwanted, unloved, unneeded.

But, even when we are despised or scorned, we can cling to the truth that our lives have purpose, and by simply being who we are, we can make a difference.

May our Creator help us see our value this day.

March 6

God sets the time for tearing down and the time for building up. ECCLESIASTES 3:3B

Like the construction of a new building, the demolition of an old building requires skill and precision. It is not done until it is clear that nothing of value will be hurt by the process. Then, on a day when the weather is right and the preparations complete, the dynamite charge is set, and the building falls in on itself. Now something new can be built.

A certain inevitability permeates our life cycles – the cycles of construction, use, destruction, and new construction. In order to build something new in our lives (beliefs or values, goals or passions, relationships or commitments), the old must often be torn down. There is a time for "tearing down and a time for building up." The tearing down process can be very painful. But it is bearable if we see it as a part of God's action in our lives, done in God's time, with our growth and well-being as its goal.

May the Source of our being provide us with strength to bear the tearing down and vision for the building up.

March 7

You will listen, O Lord, to the prayers of the lowly; you will give them courage. PSALM 10:17

Some of us begin the process of spiritual recovery needing to forget our notions of our own power, our own ability to control or fix our lives. For others of us, the beginning is different. We have grown up with a deeply embedded sense of personal powerlessness. We set ourselves up to be victims over and over again because we do not believe we have the power or strength to be anything else.

For those of us who approach life convinced of our powerlessness, the path to spiritual recovery begins with the principle embodied in the Second Step: the belief that a power greater than ourselves cares about us, listens to us, and will give us courage and strength to work toward wholeness. Recognizing that we have been living a self-destructive life, we can claim the power we have: the power to take our lives in our hands and turn them over to God. We have the power to make the decision that we will work toward our own well-being.

May God lift us up and give us courage.

March 8

It is better to have only a little, with peace of mind, than be busy all the time with both hands, trying to catch the wind. ECCLESIASTES 4:6

The writer is not criticizing hard work as such, or even busyness. He is cautioning us against the kind of obsessive behavior that drives us toward illusive, false goals. Success for its own sake is such a goal, as is wealth for its own sake, or popularity or power or happiness.

These symbols of achievement, like the wind, are not in themselves bad. The problem comes when we make them our goal, our purpose for living, the focus of all our energies. Then we find ourselves living a trapped life of compulsive work for elusive goals.

Many of us involved in the Twelve-Step program tend toward compulsive behavior of one kind or another. Hard work or self-sacrifice are socially approved, which makes them easy to justify. We need to help each other continually call into question our goals and the means we use to attain them.

May our Deliverer rescue us from compulsive effort toward elusive goals.

March 9

You, Lord, are all I have, and you give me all I need; my future is in your hands. PSALM 16:5

Our reason tells us over and over again that worrying about what lies ahead is foolish. And we know that imagining all of the worst things that could happen to us is time wasted. But still we do it, borrowing trouble from tomorrow and letting it destroy our serenity today.

The psalmist in this verse lays out the concepts undergirding the Third Step. We make a decision to trust God with our future. We turn our lives over to God, not so that we will no longer be responsible, but so that God can direct us down the path of responsible living. Sometimes that path involves planning for the future. Sometimes it involves playing out in our minds what we fear most so as to defuse that fear. But always it involves recognition that what lies ahead is in the hands of our God who is, finally, all we can count on and who wants to give us all we need.

May we be given the courage to put our lives in God's open hands.

March 10

Everyone who lives ought to be wise; it is as good as receiving an inheritance and will give you as much security as money can. ECCLESIASTES 7:11–12A

How much easier our lives would be if only everyone were wise, everyone had common sense, everyone behaved responsibly. We would never have to be angered by another's stupidity, never hurt by another's thoughtlessness, never inconvenienced by another's carelessness. If only. . . .

But . . . we face the truth. If *we* were wise, we would realize that no one can make us angry. Anger is our own response to a painful situation. We would know that in many cases others do not have the power to hurt us unless we give them that power. We would see the behavior of others as opportunity, not inconvenience.

If we were wise, we would begin taking responsibility for our own lives instead of blaming God and others for our trouble. We would ask God to begin developing in us wisdom, compassion, and self-respect. These gifts are more valuable than anything money can buy.

May God fill us with wisdom.

March 11

You save those who are humble, but you humble those who are proud. PSALM 18:27

Some of us discover through the Fourth Step a certain pride or arrogance at the core of our personalities. We maintain the childish perspective that we are the center of the universe and everything should revolve around us. Our frustrations, resentments, and angers are usually directed at those persons or institutions that refuse to comply.

For others of us, Fourth-Step reflection brings forth a realization that we have always seen ourselves on the fringe, never in the center. We orbit around another power, never taking control of our lives, never recognizing our own gravitational pull. To us, God says, "You are the center of your life. You are unique and wonderful and filled with potential."

God wants us to see ourselves as God sees us. We are one very tiny and insignificant part of an incredibly complicated created order. Yet, at the same time, we are individually and intimately treasured by our Creator. Doing the Fourth Step can help bring balance into our vision of ourselves.

May our Creator give us the humility to look honestly at ourselves.

March 12

So I realized that all we can do is be happy and do the best we can while we are still alive. ECCLESIASTES 3:12

Is it possible to be happy as a matter of choice? Or is the writer implying a cause and effect relationship in this verse — I will be happy when I am doing the best that I can? Or perhaps, I will do the best I can when I am happy.

Whichever way one interprets the verse, there is an underlying assumption of self-knowledge. In order to know whether we are doing our best, we need to have some awareness of what we can do, and a deep acceptance of our limits. Much of the unhappiness we bring upon ourselves comes from unrealistic self-expectation. We want not to be the best we can be, but to be the best. We measure ourselves and continually come up lacking — and therefore unhappy — because our measuring stick is derived not from our own potential but from what we see in others. We fall short and slide into the quicksand of self-deprecation and self-pity. When we accept ourselves for who we are, doing the best we can and being happy go hand in hand.

May the Source of our lives help us accept our limits and live to our fullest.

March 13

The Lord rewards me because I do what is right.
PSALM 18:20A

One of the greatest rewards we can have for doing what is right is the knowledge that we did, in fact, do something right. God wants us to have that joy. God gives us the privilege of making judgments about ourselves so that in many cases we will be able to say, "Yes, in this instance, I made a good choice." "Yes, when this happened, I responded in a constructive way."

When dealing with ourselves as well as with others, it is important to never let negative thoughts and observations overpower the positive. In fact, God offers us forgiveness, so that good feelings about self can always dominate and energize us.

An experience common to persons actively walking a spiritual path has been described by some as the lifting of a fog or the breaking of dawn. Others talk of feeling new life, new energy. Whatever the image, it is God's gift to us — the gift of seeing ourselves as good, valuable, and loveable.

May God give us this gift today.

March 14

Listen before you answer. If you don't, you are being stupid and insulting. PROVERBS 18:13

When we respond without listening for both facts and feelings, without listening with both our minds and our hearts, we are selling ourselves short. But we are also insulting the other in a variety of ways.

Jumping in with a diversion is like saying, "I don't think what you are saying is important or that you are important." Proposing a solution is as much as saying, "I think you are too stupid to figure this out for yourself." Quickly pointing out the other's fault is as much as saying, "You certainly are incapable of handling your own life." Topping the other's story is a direct way of saying, "Your problems are insignificant compared to mine." When we respond without really listening, our response reflects our lack of concern and respect for the other.

To listen with mind and heart is to say, "I care about you. You are important. I believe you are capable of handling your own life."

May God give us listening ears and listening hearts.

March 15

No one can see his or her own errors; deliver me, Lord, from hidden faults! PSALM 19:12

In this verse, the psalmist reflects one of the problems we have in doing the Fourth Step, and gives us a prayer for our Fifth Step. No matter how careful our inventory, no matter how honest our confession, there will always be parts of self that remain hidden or are interpreted inaccurately. For this reason, the best Fourth Steps are those done with the guidance of a wise friend or sponsor, someone who will question our assumptions, who will keep us probing deeper and deeper.

But, even the best Fourth Step leaves much uncovered, so as we move on to the Fifth Step – confession to God and another person the exact nature of our wrongs – we need humility. It is important to admit there is much in our lives that is still hidden – some things that will surface later, and other things that will, likely, remain buried in our subconscious. So, we admit that we cannot know everything and ask our Maker to forgive us for our hidden faults, and deliver us from them.

May our Maker deliver us from hidden faults.

March 16

But the joy you have given me is more than they will ever have with all their grain and wine. PSALM 4:7

You can tell happiness by a smile or a laugh. But joy, real joy, is something else, something that only the eyes reveal. There is a softness and gentleness to those eyes. When they look at you, you feel accepted and affirmed even though no words are spoken. They seem to look out and in at the same time, loving both self and other, judging neither.

When we meet such persons, we want to touch them, to reach out and feel their faces or arms as if somehow in the touching the joy they have will flow to us. And they allow us to touch them, both face and heart. They can live with a kind of abandon because they know the source of their joy.

We want to be like them, but they want us to be ourselves, to travel our own path, to experience our own sorrow, to grow and deepen in our own way. We cannot, through an act of will, be joyful. But we can move ahead in our spiritual journey so that we will be ready to accept joy when it is given and let it flow through us to others.

May our Helper prepare us to receive the gift of joy.

March 17

May my words and my thoughts be acceptable to you, O Lord, my refuge and my redeemer! PSALM 19:14

What a difference it makes that this prayer is addressed to our redeemer and not to our judge. If we were trying to be acceptable to a judge, all of the burden would be on us. We would need to make ourselves acceptable, come to the judge without any imperfections. But God is our redeemer, the one who accepts us as we are and then works to make our words and thoughts and actions acceptable.

The Sixth Step calls upon us to be ready to have God remove our shortcomings one by one. The active part of the process for us is being ready, entirely ready. We need to clean from our hearts and minds any desire to hold onto self-destructive or counterproductive ways of thinking and acting. These negative qualities have been our companions for a long time. We know how they feel and can anticipate the response of others. To be ready to have these qualities removed is a major, often frightening, step. We enter the unknown with only the promise that our God wants to make us whole.

May our Redeemer find us ready for a new way of living.

March 18

Keep me safe, also, from willful sins; don't let them rule over me. PSALM 19:13A

The psalmist must have had some sense of the power addictive behavior has over a person. We are ruled by a desire for something—alcohol, other drugs, food, sex, money, security, relationships. What appears to the outsider to be a simple choice is, in fact, a deep struggle between our will to live whole, healthy lives and our will to destroy ourselves. And the social and personal ramifications of a lost battle are great.

In those areas of addiction, the opposing forces have almost equal strength. It is foolhardy to try to do battle alone, especially when our Deliverer, the one who grieves every time we lose a battle, has promised to help if we ask. Our Creator has promised to keep us safe from that part of our will that is working against us. The Seventh Step calls us to ask our Deliverer for help.

Trying to do battle without relying on others who are veterans, who have waged the same battles we are waging and who can give us reinforcement and hope, is also risky and seldom necessary.

May our Deliverer keep us safe in the battle.

March 19

Whatever it is in your power to do, do with all your might. For there is no action, no reasoning, no learning, no wisdom in the world of the dead where you are going. ECCLESIASTES 9:10

On our spiritual journey, we have attempted to sort out what is in our power to do and what is not. And we have tried to let go of all the physical and emotional activities that are not in our control and that drain us of our energy. Once we have accomplished the task of letting go, the words of the writer of Ecclesiastes can ring in our ears: "Whatever you can do, do with all your might."

There is nothing timid or reticent about our stride when we are walking with God. We can approach life with energy and zest, focusing on all that we can do to make our lives better and consequently to enrich and empower the lives of those around us.

There will come a time when our abilities to learn and to do will diminish, and then there will come the time when they will be gone. But while we are still able, our goal is to discover all that we can do, and then do it with all our might.

May God bless us with energy to do all we can do.

March 20

You have not let my enemies capture me; you have given me freedom to go where I wish. PSALM 31:8

A sense of joyous victory rings through this verse. God has not let our enemies – those forces both internal and external that work against us – capture us. We have discovered the true nature of ourselves, both the good and the bad, and have asked God to remove our shortcomings. Once our shortcomings are removed, our strengths are inevitably enhanced.

For many of us, what seems to be a natural next step is to reflect back on our past lives. We think about the important relationships we have had and how our past attitudes or behavior might have hurt those persons and the relationships. At this stage of our recovery, it feels good to honestly ask, whom have I hurt? We do not need to be afraid of the question anymore because we know that we are new people with a new strength. God has given us our lives back so we can live the very best way possible. One positive step we can take, the Eighth Step, is to make a list of those we have harmed and be willing to make amends.

May God guide us as we live in freedom.

March 21

Teach me Lord, what you want me to do. PSALM 28:11A

The woman realized that through the years she had consciously and unconsciously dwelt on the negative behavior of others, criticizing them freely, and then setting herself up as a model of competence and integrity.

But, when the woman began looking at herself honestly, she realized that her need for adoration was not a healthy need and was being satisfied at the expense of others. Her behavior was hurting her relationships both with self and with others.

The woman began to focus on herself, her own strengths and weaknesses, her own dis-ease, and a great burden was lifted from those around her. That action was, in and of itself, an amend for her past destructive behavior. But she wanted to do more, so she began looking at others with new eyes, seeing what was good in them, talking about it, building up instead of tearing down.

May our Helper teach us what we should do to make amends.

March 22

What you say can preserve life or destroy it; so you must accept the consequences of what you say. PROVERBS 18:21

How often have we had that sick feeling in the pit of our stomachs when we realized that we have said a cruel, thoughtless, or cutting word, and that nothing we can do can take it back.

The automatic response to such situations is to build ourselves a fort of self-justification and rationalization. We are experts at finding excuses for our ill-conceived words. But, while a fort might protect us from some of the consequences of our words, it creates any number of negative consequences itself. Other people are blocked out. We are left alone.

As we work toward spiritual wholeness, we develop the ability to catch ourselves quickly when we find ourselves building walls of self-justification. We stop and admit to self and the one hurt, "I made a mistake. Can you forgive me?" By doing this, even words with destructive potential can be preservers of life, deepening our relationships with ourselves and with others.

May the Source of all life use our words to preserve life.

March 23

I feel completely secure, because you protect me from the power of death. PSALM 16:9B–10A

In the Hebrew wisdom literature, the word *death* sometimes refers to actual, physical death. More often it refers to a living death, the kind of life so filled with fear, anger, pain, resentment, obsessions, or other qualities that cut us off from loving relationships with self and others, that we cannot really live. In a living death we are alive in body but dead in spirit.

These forces of death are powerful, so powerful that it takes persistence and the help of a higher power to be safe from them. It is not enough to ask God to remove them once and for all. If we are not diligent, they will creep back into our lives and begin choking off all that is good.

The daily inventory suggested by the Tenth Step helps us note not only our strengths but also those places where we need help. Whenever we recognize a weakness, we can quickly begin working on it, trusting that God will help us. In this way, we remain secure from the power of death.

May our Protector keep us from a living death.

March 24

Let your father and mother be proud of you; give your mother that happiness. PROVERBS 23:25

This verse speaks to us both as children of parents and parents of children. The writer recognizes the responsibility children have to their parents – and to themselves – to try in whatever way they can to live lives that are constructive. This involves listening to advice, learning from mistakes, treating others and self with respect and dignity.

As parents, we are called upon to set aside our own expectations for what our children should be and do and accept our children's life choices unless they are clearly self-destructive. Many people live out their lives trying to gain parental approval, but that gift is not given because the child does not measure up to the parents' expectations. Accepting our children for what they are, looking for the good even during difficult times, and being proud of them at each stage of their lives is one of the greatest gifts we can give them.

May God strengthen and bless the parent/child relationships in our lives.

March 25

Don't make friends with people who have hot, violent tempers. You might learn their habits and not be able to change. PROVERBS 22:24-25

The writer of the proverb stops with one example—"Hot, violent tempers"—but we could add many other qualities that are contagious. Like the common cold, the virus of negative behavior tends to infect us easily. We pick up dishonesty, the tendency to rationalize, contempt for others, self-pity, envy, intolerance, selfishness, cynicism, vindictiveness, and many other qualities from those with whom we associate.

But the responsibility is clearly ours. We do not need to make friends with persons who will likely have a negative impact on us. We do not need to nurture friendships when it becomes clear that they are not good for us. And we can try not to take on the negative qualities of those who might influence us. The problem is that we cannot see with clarity the ways in which we are being influenced.

The good news is that positive qualities are also contagious. Our choice of friendships can help us in our struggle for spiritual health and wholeness.

May the Source of health bless us with good friends.

March 26

Some trust in their war chariots and others trust in horses, but we trust in the power of the Lord our God.
PSALM 20:7

Some trust in money, others in education. Some trust in family, others in themselves. Some trust in contacts, others in status. Some trust in reason, others in instinct.

But we, we trust in the power of our God. The power of God is like the diesel fuel for a truck. There is much we must do to keep our truck running: check the tires, turn on the ignition, let out the clutch, shift, steer, brake. But without the fuel we can go nowhere.

The Eleventh Step tells us a way to fuel our tanks—through prayer and meditation. Prayer and meditation are like pulling off the road, getting away from the traffic and confusion of our lives, and stretching our legs. It is a time when God—who wants to see us traveling forward, able to carry heavy loads, secure in our sense of purpose—can fill us with pure energy.

May our Creator fill us with energy for the journey.

March 27

Riches will do you no good on the day you face death, but honesty can save your life. PROVERBS 1:4

It seems clear from the context that the writer of this proverb had in mind a living death—those situations in life that like weeds can drag us down and choke off our sense of being alive and well. In such situations, a person rich in money or property or education or family heritage will stand as naked as the poorest person. Any person's spirit can be battered by certain life experiences.

At these times, the only quality that can help us is honesty—an honest admission of our powerlessness, an honest acceptance of our responsibility, an honest reaching out to God and to others for help.

"Life"—living that is built with self-respect and love, that is energized by meaning and belonging, that is content with the day and hopeful for the future—this kind of living God sets on the firm foundation of honesty.

May the Source of life set our lives on the foundation of honesty.

March 28

Remember the Lord in everything you do, and God will show you the right way. PROVERBS 3:6

The Book of Proverbs has a delightful, everyday practicality about it. God is an interacting being involved in the day to day. God is not concerned with just the big issues of faith and salvation but about the decisions we make – and the connections we make with each other – every day.

The writer makes it clear that the reason God is concerned and involved is not so that God can judge us and punish us when we fail, but because God is for us. God is our lifeblood. God wants all that is best for us.

Remembering this God in everything we do is the ultimate statement of love and hope for ourselves. We can now begin to put behind us all that is destructive (the compulsions, the addictions, the perfectionism, the attempts to control, the guilt, the shame) and step out with a new sense of our own worth. If God is for us, then we can be for ourselves. If God is concerned about our wholeness, then surely we can work toward our own health.

May God guide us and bless us.

March 29

I will tell my people what you have done; I will praise you in their assembly. PSALM 22:22

Why do we sometimes find it easy to sit at a meeting and talk openly about God's work in our lives, but when it comes to talking to our families, we tighten up?

Perhaps we have tried to talk and have gotten a negative response. The people who know us best have been so manipulated and hurt by our behavior through the years that now they hear a built-in judgment when we suggest they may need the same help we needed. Or they see unspoken manipulation in our words, another attempt to control their lives by subtly suggesting a course of action ("It worked for me, it can work for you").

The Twelfth Step states that we should practice the principles we have learned in all our affairs, and one of the most basic of these principles is to let go of the deep need to control the lives of those we love. Once they see in us a way of life they admire and once they know we are no longer attempting to control them, they may ask to hear our story, and then it will be the right time to tell. Until then, our "telling" must be in the way we live.

May our Creator make of our lives a message to those we love.

March 30

Happy are those who reject the advice of evil people, who do not follow the example of sinners or join those who have no use for God. PSALM 1:1

The Psalmist seems to assume that we not only can but should determine who is evil and avoid those persons. When we turn verses such as this into prescriptions (In order to be happy you must . . .), we find we are continually making judgments about others and therefore about their suggestions or examples.

How different our response is if we see the statement as an observation, not a prescription. The psalmist may well have noted that persons who are going through a happy time in life are those who have rejected poor advice or bad examples.

The principles of the Twelve Steps help us keep our focus on ourselves, on our own inventory. By praying daily for guidance for our lives, we can see ourselves as persons treasured and loved by God and see others as persons we accept and love without necessarily following their example.

May God bless us with hearts that accept others.

March 31

Keep your temper under control. It is foolish to harbor a grudge. ECCLESIASTES 7:9

The problem of what to do with anger is age-old. The writer of Ecclesiastes sets up extreme responses. One extreme is the burst of temper, the out-of-control rage. Another extreme is holding your anger, nurturing your resentment, harboring a grudge. When we fly off the handle, we release our own emotion at the expense of another and usually make a bad situation worse. But when we hold our tongue, hang onto the hurt that provoked the anger, let it simmer and fester, that anger becomes like acid, burning us up from the inside. And, of course, it also seriously affects the relationship we have with the person who hurt us and provoked our anger in the first place.

Finding some middle ground, some way to release anger constructively, is one of the most important tasks we have. One helpful hint is to always remember that anger is a signal that something else has happened—pain, hurt, embarrassment, humiliation. Naming the feeling and talking it out helps defuse the anger and restore the relationship.

May God help us find constructive ways of handling anger.

april

April 1

The road the righteous travel is like the sunrise, getting brighter and brighter until the daylight has come. PROVERBS 4:18

When the family traveled with their small children, they always arose before the dawn. Tiptoeing in the dark, they carried their sleeping children into the car and set out. As they drove, the darkness turned to dawn, and then dawn to the full light of day.

Our spiritual journeys often begin the same way. It is dark and cold, but we set out anyway, trusting that the dawn will come, and we will have a clearer vision of the road ahead. It is easy to stumble in that early morning darkness, easy to decide it is not worth it and go back to bed, easy to give up on the journey.

It is at these times that we can reach out to the community of journeyers around us, especially to those who have already experienced the coming of dawn. We can hold out our hands and ask for help, knowing that by so doing we will become part of a chain of help. Soon our other hand will be clasped by someone else who is reaching out just as we have done.

May our Protector guide us during the early morning darkness.

April 2

May my enemy's life soon be ended; may another take his job! May his children be homeless beggars; may they be driven from the ruins they live in! PSALM 109:8, 10

The psalmist seems filled with the desire for revenge, the need to get even. He wants all those who have hurt him punished—even their children. The Book of Psalms is, in fact, filled with prayers asking God to punish harshly those who have hurt us.

Behind these prayers is the legitimate observation that there are times when the behavior of others has a very destructive effect on our lives. No matter how much we try to respond constructively, the reality is that others can and do make our lives very difficult and painful at times.

What God is telling us is that it is all right to want to see wrongdoers punished, but the punishment needs to be left to God. Resentment and the desire to get even are natural human emotions, but they will destroy us if we continue to hold onto them or carry them out ourselves. We need to turn them over to God in trust.

May we grow toward trusting God's justice.

April 3

I have lived too long with people who hate peace! I am for peace; but when I speak, they are for war.
PSALM 120:6–7

In this psalm the writer is pleading with God to help him live peacefully in a nation that values war over peace and makes life very difficult for those persons who treasure peace.

But the struggle is often much closer to home. As we concentrate on the spiritual dimensions of our lives, seeking both inner peace and harmonious relationships, we sometimes feel beset on every side by people who want war. These people may criticize, taunt, goad, or ridicule. They may deliberately behave in unacceptable ways, waiting for us to respond in anger, needing us to act as they are acting. It is human nature to want people in our worlds to reflect whatever is inside of us, whether that is harmony or dissonance.

One of our most difficult spiritual struggles is to learn to detach ourselves from the behavior of those people and still love them. As soon as we respond in frustration, anger, or hate, we find our own inner harmony gone, replaced by dissonance.

May the Creator of all give us power to detach with love.

April 4

Do not stay away from me! Trouble is near, and there is no one to help. PSALM 22:11

The psalmist in this verse reflects the principal thought in both Steps One and Two: Trouble is near. It is all around me, it is within me, and there is no one to help. I cannot help myself, and others have failed me. Where am I to turn?

The psalmist turns to God, to a power beyond self, a power greater than anything we can imagine. He pleads with God not to stay away but to come, to be with him and help. The Second Step talks about the restoration of sanity. We do not like to admit that our behavior has not been sane. But irrational behavior is the inevitable by-product of living with our own addictions and the addictions of others. We become a little crazy — we hurt ourselves, we hurt others. Our behavior is more counterproductive than productive, our words more negative than positive, our thoughts more destructive than creative.

Restoration of sanity has to do with being turned around, so that we can work *for* self and not against self.

May the Highest Power work to restore our lives.

April 5

The more easily you get your wealth, the less good it will do you. PROVERBS 20:21

For those living in poverty, it is hard to believe that wealth is not something that is always worth having no matter how one gets it. But those who have plenty know that money can work for you or against you – it is not always good. And there seems often to be a link between how easily wealth is acquired and how much good it does. In the long run, few people profit emotionally and spiritually from winning a lottery or inheriting a fortune.

The quick fix, like quick money, is rarely advantageous in the long run. We all want to avoid hard work, struggle, suffering, growing pains, learning experiences. We want maturity, wisdom, and serenity, but we do not want to pay the price. We look for the easy path, the downhill road. But God knows we need to trudge uphill, to take risks, to make mistakes, to suffer, to cry out for help, to respond to the cries around us. The worthwhile life is often difficult, but our Creator and Helper has promised to be with us.

May our Helper uphold us along the difficult paths.

April 6

Some people have hot tempers. Let them take the consequences. If you get them out of trouble once, you will have to do it again. PROVERBS 19:19

The writer has observed a certain inevitability in life. There are consequences for bad behavior. And we know, if we stop to think about it, that this is a good thing. We would be much less mature, much less wise if, no matter what we did, things turned out all right.

But sometimes we forget this when dealing with those we love. We want to protect them from the consequences of their behavior. We do not want them to suffer, be publicly shamed, or have their lives disrupted. So we run defense, we cover up, we rationalize, we blame others, we do whatever we can to disrupt the natural flow from behavior to consequence. We may even think we are doing the loving thing. But we are actually blocking the growth and maturity of our loved ones. It may seem heartless at the time, but we need to step back, detach, and let our loved ones learn from their own mistakes.

May the Creator of all give us faith that our loved ones are being cared for.

April 7

Even if I go through the deepest darkness, I will not be afraid, Lord, for you are with me. Your shepherd's rod and staff protect me. PSALM 23:4

The Third Step (turning our wills and our lives over to the care of God) reflects the message of the Twenty-third Psalm. God is our shepherd, our guide, our protector during all times in our lives. But this particular verse concentrates on the dark times, times when death of body or spirit hovers close. There is no attempt by the psalmist to say we will never have those times, that we will be spared darkness and death—our own or that of those close to us.

God's promise is to protect us from the power that death has—the power to instill fear in us and keep us from trusting our shepherd. It is impossible to help a trapped sheep unless that sheep trusts the person trying to help. If the sheep panics and struggles, it works toward its own destruction. But when the sheep knows its shepherd, fear vanishes and the shepherd can lift the sheep with strong arms and save it.

May we find in God a loving shepherd during our darkest times.

April 8

There is a right time and a right way to do everything, but we know so little! ECCLESIASTES 8:6

There is a wonderful story in Genesis about Joseph, who was sold into slavery by his brothers. He becomes the ruler of Egypt, and his brothers are forced by famine to depend on him for their sustenance. After their father's death, the brothers are afraid that Joseph will punish them, but he says, "You plotted evil against me, but God turned it into good, in order to preserve the lives of many. . . ." At many points in this story, God was able to take bad decisions and use them for good.

Knowing this gives us great freedom and humility. We will never have available all the information we need to make a sound choice. But we have a God we can trust, a God who is powerful enough to guide us toward good choices. And when we make mistakes—decisions based on ignorance, fear, anger, envy, selfishness, or misinformation—we have a God who can use them for our own good and the good of others.

May we feel free to take risks, trusting that God will use them for good.

April 9

Never let yourselves think that you are wiser than you are; simply obey the Lord and refuse to do wrong.
PROVERBS 3:7

This verse implies that it is simple to obey, to know right from wrong, to always be able to decide what is best. Sometimes it *is* simple. God has provided us with a wealth of guidelines for decision making that make some choices easy. But the more complicated our lives are – the more relationships we are involved in, the more active we are, the more we are trying to affect change in the world – the more difficult our choices become.

If someone needs our help, God's guidance makes it clear that we are to help. But what if helping one person involves ignoring or hurting another? What do we do when time spent with spiritual journeyers in a Twelve-Step group means time away from our families who need us? One of the realities of living in an imperfect world is that many of our choices are between the greater of goods or the lesser of evils. The best we can do is to establish doing good as a priority and then trust God's power to redeem all our choices.

May our Helper help us in our difficult decisions.

April 10

Lord, who may enter your Temple? A person whose words are true and sincere, and who does not slander others. PSALM 15:2B–3A

The almost automatic response to trouble in our lives is to find fault in others and then publicly decry them for their failures.

Sometimes we blame individuals within the legal system, seeing nothing but harassment and oppression. Sometimes in anger we strike out against a teacher or principal because of the problems we or our children are having in school. Sometimes in frustration we attack clergy or members of our church or synagogue, blaming them for being weak or ineffective in helping us. And the people closest to us, the people we love, are often the first targets of our blame.

All institutions, helping professionals, friends, and family members are imperfect. None can solve our problems. Finally, we need to quit blaming and look to ourselves. What is my pain? In what ways have I made it worse? In what ways can I help myself? What must be turned over to God?

May the Source of our being give us insights as we search ourselves for strengths and weaknesses.

April 11

The road of the wicked is dark as night. They fall, but cannot see what they have stumbled over. PROVERBS 4:19

The Book of Proverbs tends to divide all people into two groups: the righteous and the wicked. Most of us would feel uncomfortable identifying with either group. We know we are not always wicked, but neither are we always righteous. We all have dark places within us, places where we stumble and cannot see what we have stumbled over.

These places are a double frustration. First of all, we cannot see the problem and so we trip over it and fall. But the bigger frustration is that even after we have fallen, we still are in the dark, unable to see what we have stumbled over. We cannot see the problem, and so we do not learn from our mistake. We just make it again and again.

At these times, we can ask for wisdom from God and honest help from our friends. What is unclear to us may be painfully clear to others. If we listen with humility and open minds to others and test their ideas, perhaps we can uncover the stumbling blocks that have remained hidden.

May the Source of life bring light to our dark places.

April 12

Someone who holds back the truth causes trouble, but one who openly criticizes works for peace. PROVERBS 10:10

While it is true that we cannot control or fix another person, we still have a responsibility to others. The difference between being responsible *for* and responsible *to* is a very important one as we grow in our own spirituality. When we feel responsible *for* another, we protect, rescue, manipulate, and control. We attempt to solve their problems and have in our minds a set of expectations that we want them to live up to. In general, we carry them as a burden.

An important part of the Twelve-Step journey is to set that burden down and begin being responsible *to* others, relating to them as competent persons capable of handling their own lives and needing to learn from their own mistakes. When we begin relating to others as peers, we can listen, encourage, share, and – when it is necessary – confront or criticize. Knowing that we are not trying to control or manipulate them, others can accept our criticism, letting it "work for peace."

May God help us let go of our sense of responsibility for others.

April 13

Give her credit for all she does. She deserves the respect of everyone. PROVERBS 31:31

This verse comes at the end of a chapter describing a wonderful wife—the sort of wife a man can hope to have if he fears God, loves Wisdom, and lives a good life. The relationship described is one of partnership, each person responsible for his or her own domain, each person encouraging the other to be the best he or she can be.

Reading about the ideal can be frustrating when we are in relationships that fall far short of that. We can turn this verse around and think, "If only he or she would give me credit for all I do. I deserve more respect than I get. I would be a better partner or friend if I were treated better."

But the point the writer is making is that we need to try to see all that is good in others, giving them credit for their strengths, showing them respect and love. Even if they do not respond in kind and we feel hurt and put down, we should resist the temptation to focus on the negative. Doing so would only postpone any chance for a relationship of mutual respect.

May our Creator give us the vision and strength to support and respect others.

April 14

Keep your promise, Lord, and forgive my sins, for they are many. PSALM 25:11

The forgiveness for our sins that God has promised is one of the greatest gifts we can be given. In our Fourth Step we became aware of the many ways in which we have failed. The Fifth Step is our chance to pour out all of these failings—and guilts—onto God and one other trusted person. The relief we feel in having all that weight off our hearts is compounded when we are told, "God forgives you. God does not hold anything against you. In God's eyes you are like a new-born infant."

The young woman had paid a high price for her behavior: loss of family and friends, degradation, imprisonment. But God had not forgotten her, and gradually her life began to turn around. Under the guidance of drug counselors, she moved through the first four Steps, and then came time for the Fifth Step. She could not believe the release she felt. For the first time since she could remember, she felt clean, new, ready to move on and rebuild her life. She had accepted God's forgiveness.

May our loving God cleanse and renew us.

April 15

Relieve me of my worries and save me from all my troubles. PSALM 25:17

When we ask God to relieve us of our worries, are we asking to be free from worrying or to have everything in our lives fixed so that we will not have to worry? For most of us, it is probably the latter. We want our partner, our children, our parents, friends, or others changed so that we will not have to be concerned about them. We want good health and financial security and all the possessions that we feel we need. Then we would not have to worry.

But worry itself is a counterproductive behavior, one we need to be ready to have God remove as a part of our Sixth Step. God wants us to be able to live in such a trust relationship with God that we can enjoy all that is good in a day, struggle with the problems of the day, and tend to our own spiritual well-being. God cares for those we love, and our lives are in God's hands. We can set aside our worries and focus on each moment, each day.

May God replace our habit of worry with a sense of being cared for.

April 16

Listen, O Lord, to my plea for justice; pay attention to my cry for help! Listen to my honest prayer. PSALM 17:1

I "humbly asked God to remove my shortcomings." There is no more honest prayer than this Seventh-Step prayer. We have admitted our shortcomings – all those attitudes and behaviors that stand as barriers between us, others, and God. By asking God to remove them, we admit our own inability to fix ourselves, and we give to a power greater than ourselves the freedom to begin changing us. This is an act of great courage, strength, and humility.

But it is not a "once and for all time act." In fact, the best way to accomplish this Step is to focus on one shortcoming at a time. For instance, we might ask God to remove our tendency to judge others and fill us with tolerance and love. It might take days or weeks or months for change to begin, but gradually we will notice that we are loving more and judging less. Then we can focus on another shortcoming, trusting that, once again, God will help us.

May God listen to our honest prayers for help in removing our shortcomings.

April 17

Forgive the sins and errors of my youth. In your constant love and goodness, remember me, Lord. PSALM 25:7

The psalmist assumes that we all have backgrounds that cause us guilt. No one grows up without thinking, saying, and doing all kinds of things that are hurtful both to self and to others. At some level of our conscious or subconscious minds, we carry all that guilt without really knowing that it is there. To receive God's forgiveness, it is enough to pray as the psalmist prays, "Forgive the sins and errors of my youth." But we usually need to do more in order to forgive ourselves so we can move on.

As we think back on our pasts, it is helpful to make a list of each person close to us, and then ask, "In what ways have I hurt that person?" Write down specific words and actions, but also try to remember attitudes that worked against your relationship, attitudes such as envy, resentment, impatience, ingratitude, intolerance. This thoughtful and honest recollection of our pasts is the Eighth Step toward spiritual recovery.

May God help us recall all those persons whom we have hurt.

April 18

Try to make a profit dishonestly, and you get your family in trouble. PROVERBS 15:27A

The writer mentions one particular activity that leads to family trouble. But there are hundreds more. In fact, there is little we do that does not somehow affect, either positively or negatively, those persons closest to us. None of us lives in isolation.

But we are caught in paradox. On the one hand, we recognize and accept responsibility for all we have done to provoke or hurt others. On the other hand, we realize that their acceptance of that hurt and their reaction to it is *not* our responsibility. If our partner responds to our coolness or anger by feeling hurt and looking elsewhere for love, his or her behavior is not our fault. If our rebellious behavior as a teenager triggered fighting between our parents, we are culpable only for our own behavior, not their response. To take responsibility for another's action is to diminish their personhood and short-circuit their maturation.

May our Highest Power help us accept that for which we are responsible and let go of all else.

April 19

The Lord is righteous and good and teaches sinners the path they should follow. PSALM 25:8

God has taught us and continues to teach us the path we should follow regardless of whether we follow it or not. That kind of steadfastness of purpose is a model for us as we set out to make amends to all those we have hurt. Our amends may be rejected or ignored. Our efforts to restore relationships may be rebuffed. Our request for forgiveness may be denied. While we hope that this will not happen, the success of our Ninth Step does not depend on the other's positive response. If the other does not respond positively, we should ask ourselves if our amends were really an attempt to manipulate the other so as to make our own lives easier. Our responsibility is to make amends in as honest and as helpful a way possible.

God not only sets a model for perseverance. Because God is righteous and good, God also teaches us how we can best make our amends. Making amends that can work toward mending people and relationships requires honesty, other-centeredness, and openness to God's teaching.

May God teach us how best to make amends.

April 20

Here is a person who lives alone. He has no child, no relative, yet he is always working, never satisfied with the wealth he has. For whom is he working so hard and denying himself any pleasure? This is useless, too—and a miserable way to live. ECCLESIASTES 4:8

We wonder after reading this verse just exactly what the author thought was so miserable about this life: the lack of close relationships, the absence of pleasure, working all the time, or never feeling satisfied. Of course all four were important, but we can learn something about ourselves if we think of how we value these four things.

Some of us like working all the time but could hardly bear life without family or friends. Others like solitude but would resent having to work all the time. Some of us would give anything to feel satisfied. Others of us use the feeling of never being satisfied as an energizer in our spiritual quest. We are all different, but we have a common core: a sense of dissatisfaction or yearning that pushes us to search for something that will give us meaning. That search can lead us away from our Source, or it can bring us home to God's waiting arms.

May the Source of all life guide us as we search for meaning for our lives.

April 21

Teach me to live according to your truth, for you are my God, who saves me. I always trust in you. PSALM 25:5

We have learned much about ourselves through our efforts to work through the Fourth through Ninth Steps. In fact, as we look back we can probably see some evidence of real change in our lives. We have likely worked hard at helping God remove our worst habits and compulsions so that they gradually have had less and less hold on us. God is, indeed, creating new people of us.

But the process is never complete. Each day is a new opportunity for change and growth – and mistakes. The Tenth Step combines steps Four through Nine by suggesting a daily inventory, a daily housecleaning so that garbage never begins piling up in the corners of our minds. We are learning how to confess and ask God to forgive and change us, and we know how to sense when we have hurt another and begin to make amends. We continue our spiritual journey, making this way of thinking and acting a habit so ingrained that it becomes our automatic response.

May the Creator of all continue to create in us.

April 22

It is better to have wise people reprimand you than to have stupid people sing your praise. ECCLESIASTES 7:5

Oh, but it is so much easier to hear praise! And it is possible to conclude that if someone sees all that is good about us, he or she could not be all that stupid. Or maybe our problem is that we cannot accept praise no matter what the source. We might think so poorly of ourselves that we question the credibility of anyone who says something good. Or we see praise as an attempt to manipulate or control, which it often is, and we set up our guard, wondering what the praise giver wants from us.

Both praising and reprimanding set up a volatile dynamic between persons that can help or hurt relationships. As giver of either, we need to exercise both caution and honesty.

As receiver, our goal is to be able to separate both praise and criticism from the speaker, evaluate them on their own merit, and then accept what can be accepted and forget the rest.

May God give us discernment as we give and receive both praise and criticism.

April 23

All who see me make fun of me; they curl their lips, they shake their heads. PSALM 22:7

The boy was returning to high school after a month of treatment for chemical dependency. Thinking of his old friends, a shiver ran down his spine. He wanted to stay clean, but how would he be able to handle their ridicule? He remembered his own attitude toward others – the names he had called them, the jokes he had made about them. Now it would be his turn, and he dreaded it more than anything else.

Ridicule is a powerful weapon, often used by those who would reduce everyone to the lowest common denominator. It can undercut our best intentions and destroy our tenuous grasp on serenity. Ridicule might be as obvious as name-calling or other verbal abuse, but it can be as subtle as a raised eyebrow, a tiny smirk, or a muffled laugh. The results are predictable – hurt, followed by rage, followed by a modification of our behavior, even if it is to our own detriment. We want to become acceptable to the one who ridicules: by doing so we become unacceptable to ourselves.

May our Deliverer free us from the power of ridicule.

April 24

So don't be too good or too wise—why kill yourself.
ECCLESIASTES 7:16

On first thought, it would seem impossible that one could be too good or too wise. And, indeed, there is nothing wrong with being as good or as wise as we can be. The problem lies in the reasons for wanting to be good and wise and in the process for attaining these qualities.

If we want to be good or wise so we can feel we are better than others or so we can accept ourselves, there is something skewed about our motivation. And if we become perfectionists—obsessed with being good or wise, continually directing our thoughts inward, constantly measuring ourselves against some standard—then we have lost our freedom.

Because many of the Twelve-Step principles lead us in this direction, we need to remember that excessiveness of any kind is destructive. Our goal is not to be good or wise but to live with the freedom to accept ourselves as we are and the desire to keep growing in our ability to love others.

May our Helper guard and keep us from excessiveness of any kind.

April 25

The Lord is my shepherd, I have everything I need.
PSALM 23:1

A good shepherd knows his sheep by name, knows what each sheep needs, and works hard to provide for each one. "The Lord is my shepherd." Even though I am one of many sheep, my shepherd is working to give me, individually, everything I need.

A good shepherd always wants what is best for his sheep. Sometimes that involves moving the sheep from one place to another. The path may be difficult and dangerous, but the shepherd is always watching for those sheep who slip and fall or get lost. Each one is important, and even if it means leaving the flock for a time to rescue a single sheep, the good shepherd will do just that.

The process of "improving our conscious contact with God" (part of the Eleventh Step) can be encouraged by thinking of God as the good shepherd, by believing that God knows where the "green pastures" are, and by trusting God to lead us there.

May the Good Shepherd provide for our every need.

April 26

God sets the time for sorrow and the time for joy, the time for mourning and the time for dancing. ECCLESIASTES 3:4

At first they only heard muffled sighs. But soon the sighs turned to gasps and finally to deep, trembling sobs as all the pain of the world melded into his own pain and washed over him. "Don't cry, Daddy," his daughter pleaded. "He needs to cry," her mother whispered as she held his head to her breast. "Tears will wash the sadness from his heart so he can feel happy again."

"A time for sorrow and a time for joy." Sorrow and joy are expressions of that which makes us most human—the capacity to love deeply, the ability to care intensely. Loving makes us vulnerable. Caring opens us to loss, and loss of any kind brings grief. But by allowing ourselves to feel and express the grief that comes to us all many times during our lives, we increase our capacity to feel. And so, when good times come, the height of the joy will equal the depth of our sorrow, and we will know what it is to be truly human.

May God bless us with times of sorrow and times of joy.

April 27

Sorrow is better than laughter; it may sadden your face, but it sharpens your understanding. ECCLESIASTES 7:3

The class was asked three questions: "Do you prefer hard times or easy times? Do you think you learn more during hard times or easy times? Do you want to grow in understanding?" The answers were predictable. Everyone wanted to grow in understanding, knew they learned more during hard times, but strongly preferred times that were easy.

Perhaps it is good that we fear hard times, or we might find ourselves consciously or unconsciously creating them so that we can grow in understanding. This is particularly true if we are persons who fear boredom more than we fear difficulties. But hard times that we make for ourselves do not teach the same kinds of lessons.

The difficult times – those times when we are forced to face ourselves, to ask the hard questions, to admit our vulnerability and powerlessness – those times will come soon enough. We do not need to create them, only to let them create and renew us.

May God use hard times as a re-creative force in our lives.

April 28

I know that your goodness and love will be with me all the days of my life; and I shall dwell in the house of the Lord as long as I live. PSALM 23:6

"I know...." The spiritual awakening referred to in the Twelfth Step has to do with the movement from "I wonder..." to "I hope..." to "I think..." to "I believe..." to, finally, "I know...." It is not that we quit having times of doubt, but it is as if the balance between doubt and knowing is finally weighted on the side of knowing. We have put our lives and our wills into God's hands over and over again, and finally we have learned to trust that there is a power greater than ourselves who is concerned for our well-being, who is working for our wholeness.

And so we can say with the psalmist, "I *know* that your goodness and love will be with me all my life," or, as one translation puts it, "will follow me...." God will be with me to catch me when I stumble, to pick me up when I fall, to tap me on the shoulder and direct me down the right paths. We live with the wonderful assurance that our lives are in God's care.

May we be brought to the point of knowing and trusting God's love.

April 29

Singing to a person who is depressed is like taking off a person's clothes on a cold day or like rubbing salt in a wound. PROVERBS 25:20

How automatic it is, especially if we are feeling good, to want to cheer up persons who are depressed. And so we sing to them by chattering. We take them out to lunch, give them advice, and do whatever we can to try to get their minds off their troubles. It may work temporarily, but the depression they feel *after* our efforts will be deeper than what they felt before. We have rubbed salt in their wounds by not taking their pain seriously, by not letting them talk, by taking it upon ourselves to fix them.

Depression is often caused by something being pushed down, depressed, within a person's subconscious. It could be grief, anger, pain, or even love. But whatever it is, relief can come only when those feelings are acknowledged, taken seriously, and expressed. The best way to be a friend to someone who is depressed is to set aside our intellect and listen with our hearts, feeling with them as they re-experience their pain, walking with them as they search for health.

May our Comforter make us sensitive to the needs of those around us.

April 30

Patient persuasion can break down the strongest resistance and can even convince rulers. PROVERBS 25:15

It would be easy to interpret this verse as "Use patient persuasion to break down the strongest resistance." In other words, it is our right and responsibility to change others, and patient persuasion is a tool we can use.

But we have learned that our responsibility is to open ourselves to change, not to change others. Our attempts to change others have not only failed but have also worked against our own serenity.

This verse is not advice or method. Rather, it reflects the reality of what can and does happen in relationships when one person steps back, quits trying to manipulate and control, and concentrates on self; when one person learns patience and tolerance, and begins honestly to accept the other for what he or she is. Only when one person does this can the other dare to let down his or her resistance. Then it is safe to look at self and reach out for help in order to change. These are the "miracle stories" we hear about in Twelve-Step groups.

May God give us patience and love for those close to us.

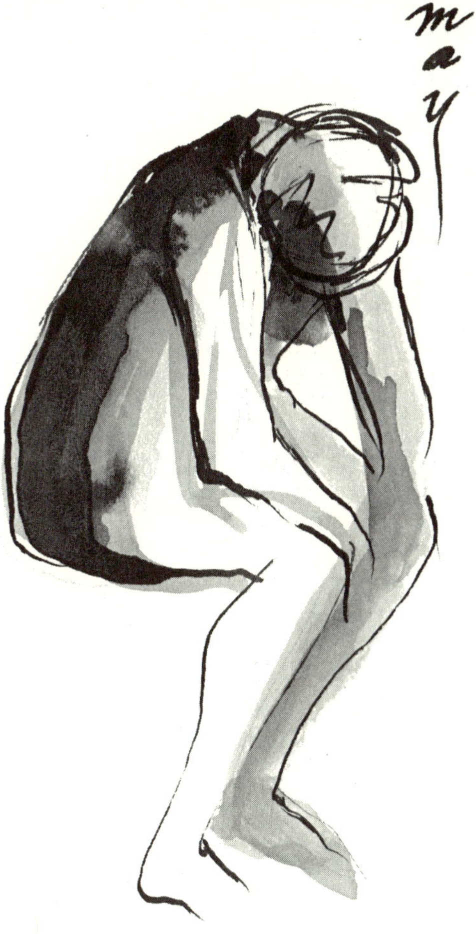
may

May 1

I can hardly see; my eyes are so swollen by weeping caused by my enemies. PSALM 6:7

The psalmist recognizes the presence of real enemies in the world, persons or forces that work against us, that seek to destroy us, that make our lives "unmanageable." What society tells us is that an enemy must either be conquered or changed in such a way that the enemy becomes a friend.

We work very hard to either defeat or fix our enemies. We scold, nag, cajole, manipulate, try to force, and threaten to desert. We try to "kill them with kindness" or shame them into changing. But somehow nothing we do ever quite works. We struggle and struggle, and our lives become more and more unmanageable.

Before we can begin our spiritual journey, we need to realize that we have taken bad advice. Attempting to defeat or fix those persons or forces in life that hurt us does not work. Accepting the futility of this advice to change others is the First Step toward spiritual recovery, a step that needs to be taken before a new way of living can be found.

May our Creator turn us toward a new way of living.

May 2

Don't be surprised when you see that the government oppresses the poor and denies them justice and their rights. ECCLESIASTES 5:8A

Even though we have a right to expect persons or institutions to do what they have agreed to do, the writer of Ecclesiastes tells us not to be surprised when they do not. Much of the frustration we experience in life could be minimized if we remembered that others are imperfect and will fall short in accomplishing their tasks.

A far more serious threat to our serenity, however, comes when we expect others to behave in ways that meet our emotional needs. We need unconditional love and affection. When our loved ones fail to meet those needs, we become angry and resentful, blaming them. We have the deep need to control. When our children or colleagues resist us, we overreact, blaming them for insolence or disobedience. Other persons are not responsible for meeting our emotional needs. Our assumption that they *are* responsible and our expectation that they *will* meet our needs cause serious rifts in our relationships and threaten our serenity.

May God replace expecting *with* accepting *in our relationships.*

May 3

. . . hide me in the shadow of your wings from the attacks of the wicked. PSALM 17:8B

Whenever danger is near, a hen with chicks will spread her wings and her chicks will run for cover, finding protection and comfort in the shadow of her wings. The psalmist pictures God as mother hen or a mother bird, instinctively wanting to protect us from all that would hurt us.

But, even as the mother hen encourages her chicks to roam freely, feeding and exploring as they will when it is safe, so God wants us to move out from under God's wings, risking, testing, exploring, and interacting with others. God wants us to grow toward maturity and use with abandon the gifts and talents we have been given, never letting fear of mistakes inhibit us.

We can live with this kind of freedom because we know that God is watching out for us, with wings spread, ready to hide us and protect us if we are in danger. But we cannot be helped if we do not listen for God's warning cries or trust God's ability to protect us.

May the protective wings of God shield us in times of danger.

May 4

Be careful how you think; your life is shaped by your thoughts. PROVERBS 4:23

It is interesting to note that the psalmist did not say, "Be careful how you feel, your life is shaped by your feelings." And yet, at times it seems as if we *are* controlled by our feelings. Anger sweeps over us and determines how we act. Despair descends on us, and the whole world looks different. Then one morning, for no particular reason, we wake up and feel good.

These feelings have no moral value; they just are. What we do with them, however, can be constructive or destructive. And that process has to do with the way we think. Do we rationalize our anger? Do we blame others when we feel hurt? Do we quit thinking about God when we feel good?

"Our lives are shaped by our thoughts." They are not changed dramatically or substantively overnight, but like a sculpture made of clay, our lives are shaped—made smooth or rough, balanced or lopsided—by our thoughts. And over them we do have control.

May the Source of life help us shape our lives with worthwhile thoughts.

May 5

Rescue me from these lions; I am helpless before these wild bulls. PSALM 22:21

The woman sat in the school counselor's office and wept as she described her attempts to make her son attend class, do his homework, behave responsibly. She had commanded, threatened, shamed, bribed, grounded, pleaded, and prayed. But nothing worked. "Do you think your son is abusing alcohol or other drugs?" the counselor asked. "Oh, no," she retorted. "He might drink, but he would never use drugs." "Alcohol is a drug—the most abused drug of all," the counselor responded quietly. Angry, the woman went home to fight her "lion" alone.

When we look at our lives carefully, we realize that there are many areas where we are helpless, where we have tried but failed. We realize that our attempts are as futile as fighting a lion alone, without weapons or help. Thank God we are not dependent on our own resources to fight the lions and wild bulls in our lives, especially the lion of our own foolish behavior.

May we turn to our Protector and others to help us in times of need.

May 6

We labor, trying to catch the wind, and what do we get? We get to live our lives in darkness and grief, worried, angry, and sick. ECCLESIASTES 5:16B–17

There are many ways we can rewrite the question so as to arrive at the writer's conclusion: We labor, trying to control our families, trying to gain happiness, trying to be successful, trying to be good. . . . Such effort inevitably leads to grief, worry, anger, or sickness. Perhaps the writer was trying to direct readers away from the assumption that anything is possessable and that attempts to get, to have, and to own are always going to end in frustration. This is true even of our serenity. Our hands must remain open, receiving serenity as a gift. If we try to grasp it, possess it, claim it as our own, it eludes us.

But how would the answer in this verse be different if the question were worded, "We *journey*, open to receiving God's gifts, and what do we get?" Such a question could lead to the answer, "We get to live our lives relaxed, accepting, challenged, and healthy."

May God help us ask the right questions.

May 7

Inexperienced people die because they reject wisdom. Stupid people are destroyed by their own lack of concern. PROVERBS 1:32

The writer points out the difference between being inexperienced and being stupid. In order to gain wisdom, an inexperienced person must either accept the wisdom others have gained or learn the hard way through his or her own experiences. We are all inexperienced in many areas of life. In order to gain wisdom, we must be willing to question and think reflectively, try to discern between the Wisdom of God and the beliefs of our culture, and develop eyes that see beyond details to the overall picture.

Persons labeled stupid by the writer are those who do not care enough to think or question, to struggle or move against the grain. They accept the easy answer, the quick fix, the shortest route, the simple solution.

For the inexperienced, growth involves accepting and learning. For the stupid, a change of heart is needed, replacing indifference with caring, apathy with concern.

May our Creator work in our lives, opening us to continue receiving wisdom.

May 8

"But now I will come," says the Lord, "because the needy are oppressed and the persecuted groan in pain. I will give them the security they long for."
PSALM 12:5

"But now I will come," says our God. "Now I *can* come." When we thought we could solve our own problems, when we assumed we could manage our own lives, when we prided ourselves on our ability to fix ourselves and others, then God could not come to us. Our doors were shut. We were going to do it ourselves.

But we have now accepted that there are many disturbing things in our lives that are out of our control. And we have recognized that our responses to situations, to others, and to our own feelings are often counterproductive. So we "groan in pain," recognizing our need for God, calling on God, deciding "to turn our will and our lives over to the care of God." This is the Third Step toward spiritual health.

Now God will come and give us the security we long for.

May our Comforter hear our cries and come to us, giving us all we need for today.

May 9

The Lord corrects those he loves, as a parent corrects a child of whom the parent is proud. PROVERBS 3:12

As children we knew instinctively the difference between correction and punishment. The difference was not so much in the actual experience as it was in the attitude of the parent. Punishment involved anger and retribution. Its purpose was as much to give vent to the frustration of the parent as it was to teach the child. When we were punished, we felt unloved, hurt, and shamed.

But correction was different. It communicated the parent's love and desire that we not hurt ourselves and that we grow to our full potential. We would usually respond with openness to correction but with anger, withdrawal, or rebellion to punishment.

God is like that loving parent, correcting us when we behave in ways that hurt ourselves or others – not to punish us or flaunt God's power, but to help us continue to grow, mature, and gain wisdom.

May we accept God's correction as a child accepts the correction of a loving parent.

May 10

It is you who light my lamp; the Lord, my God, lights up my darkness. PSALM 18:28

Doing the Fourth Step, the fearless moral inventory, is like walking around a dark room lighting one small candle at a time. Each flame gives you enough light to see the next candle. Little by little, the light spreads to even the darkest corners. When we begin lighting up this room of our lives, we discover all kinds of things we had not known before, some good and some bad. There is a crack in the wall, a floorboard missing, nails sticking out, old papers and garbage lying in a heap. But there are also areas already neat and decorated with beautiful, hand-carved wood, and corners filled with potential just waiting for a creative touch.

Our Creator desires to give us light to see ourselves because it is as harmful to leave what is good in the darkness as it is to hide what is bad. Our spiritual journey is dependent on this kind of honest knowledge of self – all that is good and all that is bad.

May the Creator of all bring light to our dark places.

May 11

Those who hide their hatred are liars. PROVERBS 10:18A

The writer is warning us that it is as easy to tell lies by what we do not say as by what we do say. If we harbor prejudices or hatred toward individuals or groups and act as if we do not, we are telling an untruth about ourselves. We are trying to make people think something about us that is not true.

Would the writer want people to go about speaking all their hatreds and prejudices? No. What he is advocating is honesty with self and others. If we recognize a prejudice, it is important to admit it, acknowledge that it is not a good thing, and try to change. Even if those negative feelings are toward someone close to us, it is better to confess them than to pretend they are not there. If we do not, the other person will sense them, and the confusion and dishonesty will do far more damage to the relationship than confession of the feelings. In fact, bringing such feelings into the open will often do much to dispel them.

May God give us the courage to be honest even about our negative feelings.

May 12

There are seven things that the Lord hates and cannot tolerate: a proud look, a lying tongue, hands that kill innocent people, a mind that thinks up wicked plans, feet that hurry off to do evil, a witness who tells one lie after another, and a person who stirs up trouble among friends. PROVERBS 6:16-19

These seven things have one thing in common: they all have to do with our relationships to others. A proud look puts down others and sets up competition and envy. A lying tongue undercuts trust. Hands, meant to nurture and help, kill instead. The intelligence we have been given so that we can make life better is used instead for thinking up wicked plans. Feet that should take us to those in need of help take us to places where we can do harm. A witness, needed to shed truth on a situation, tells lies and destroys another's chance for justice. And people who should be working for peace and harmony instead work to disrupt relationships.

From these verses we get a picture of a God who is deeply concerned about the way we live in relationship to others, who wants all our connections with others to be good, to be god-like.

May God be present in all our relationships.

May 13

Look at my affliction and suffering, and forgive all my sins. PSALM 25:18

Guilt is a killer. It can destroy our health and well-being and undermine our relationships. Guilt is often an indication that we have failed in some way, that we have not lived up to our own expectations. While such guilt indicates a certain failure, it also indicates moral good. We would not feel guilty if we had no standards. We would not suffer from guilt if we did not care about ourselves and others. So guilt is inevitable for imperfect persons who are trying to live loving, responsible lives.

But even though guilt is inevitable and is a sign that there is much that is good about us, still, it is a killer, and we need to work to get rid of it. It does no good to tell ourselves that we should not feel guilty when we have failed in some way. Neither does it help to try to convince ourselves that what we did was not really wrong and that the other person deserved it anyway. We can only be freed from guilt by admitting the wrong, confessing to God and the person we hurt, and asking for forgiveness.

May God forgive us all our sins and relieve our distress.

May 14

So they are punished by their own evil and are hurt by their own violence. PSALM 7:16

A certain common wisdom is reflected in this verse. We sow what we reap. We sleep in the bed we make. In other words, the bad things that happen to us are the predictable results of our own bad choices. We get what we deserve.

This is often true, but there are times in our lives when we know deep within us that nothing we have done is so bad that we deserve what is happening to us. We stand before God claiming our innocence and demanding an explanation for what is happening. And the only way God answers us is through a friend reaching out to help or a stranger touching us with words of comfort.

We call these people angels because they bring us God's message of love and hope during times when nothing makes any sense and when there is no reason to hope. Persons involved in a spiritual journey become part of a network of angels, touching and being touched, helping and being helped, loving and being loved.

May God use us as angels to touch others in meaningful ways.

May 15

Into your hand I entrust my spirit; you redeem me, O Lord, faithful God. PSALM 31:5

The man walked into the watch repair shop and handed the employee a beautiful, antique gold watch. He waited for the diagnosis, hoping against hope that the watch could be repaired. Then he smiled broadly as he heard the words, "This is a classic watch. We can have it in good running order in no time." But rather than leaving the watch to be fixed, he put it in his pocket and walked out.

The Fourth and Fifth Steps are like a diagnosis. We have made the effort to find what needs to be repaired, what needs to be replaced, what only needs a little polishing, and what is in good running order. But, it is not enough to know what is wrong or that we are repairable, any more than it was enough for the man with the watch to know. We need to be ready to place our prized possession—ourselves—in the care of one who has the power and expertise to help us. It is an act of will and an act of great trust in our Creator who has faithfully led us this far and wants to continue with us in our spiritual journey.

May we be ready to place ourselves in our Creator's loving care.

May 16

God sets the time for making love and the time for not making love, the time for kissing and the time for not kissing. ECCLESIASTES 3:5

We were created as sexual beings with bodies, and God saw that it was good. We were made with a longing to be held and caressed that begins in infancy and lasts a lifetime. We have needs both for physical intimacy and for erotic sexuality. Throughout our lives we are in situations where we must make careful choices about how best to satisfy each of these needs.

We may have made choices that proved to be destructive because we confused our need for intimacy with our need for sexuality. Or our choices may have led to pain because they were hasty or poorly thought out, involving no commitment or responsibility. For whatever reasons, poor choices regarding our sexuality often carry a high personal and social price tag.

The desire of our Creator for us is that our choices reflect divine timing. In that way we will receive the intimacy we need, and our sexuality can be a source of great joy and satisfaction.

May our Creator guide us as we seek to satisfy our needs for intimacy and sexuality.

May 17

Yet you made people inferior only to yourself; and crowned them with glory and honor. PSALM 8:5

When we are feeling as if the world is a dog-eat-dog place, when we see life as a jungle where only the strongest and meanest survive, when we look at others and see only pettiness and selfishness, these words of the psalmist seem absurd. How could it be that people are the height of creation, that they are "crowned with glory and honor"?

It is true that the world is an imperfect place, a place that must bring God grief. And yet the way we see things often is more a reflection of what is inside of us than what is outside of us. The old saying, "It takes one to know one," makes sense.

As we continue in our spiritual journey, one of the by-products of having our own shortcomings removed is that more and more we will begin to see both what is good in ourselves *and* what is good in others. Such vision is generative, helping ourselves and others grow toward full, connected, serene lives.

May our Helper give us eyes to see what is good in ourselves and others.

May 18

But you do see; you take notice of trouble and suffering and are always ready to help. PSALM 10:14A

This verse comes at the end of a long litany of anger and frustration. The psalmist has noticed, as we have noticed, that there is much injustice and evil in the world and that innocent people are often hurt, and he calls upon God to punish the wicked. After getting all that off his chest, it is as if his vision changes, and he begins to see what is good. He sees God at work in the world, helping those who need help.

The Seventh Step is our call to God for help. We are sick of living lives of trouble and suffering, and we have discovered how many times we have contributed to our own pain by the way we think and act. We cannot take on the rest of our world, but we can begin, today, working on ourselves. God has seen our trouble and suffering. The Source of all life knows what we need and is ready to help. We need only "humbly ask God to remove our shortcomings." And God will begin and will continue as long as we keep asking – and even sometimes when we do not.

May the Source of life continue to work in us.

May 19

The more you worry, the more likely you are to have bad dreams. ECCLESIASTES 5:3A

We have all, likely, discovered the truth of this statement. Worry not only destroys the serenity of our days, but it infects our nights, also. Worry is generally rooted in our fear that we lack control, lack power, and lack security. But while we fear that this might be true, we have not deeply accepted its truth. We wring our hands and tear our hair and think of all that could go wrong. Then we mentally play through a thousand plans for circumventing disaster.

If at this point in our spiritual journey we are still struggling with worry, perhaps we need to go back to the beginning and carefully sort out where in our lives we have power and where we do not. By truly accepting our powerlessness in certain areas of our lives and turning those areas over to God, we can take giant strides toward loosening worry's grip on us.

"May God grant us the serenity to accept the things we cannot change."

May 20

Like people who would mock a cripple, they glared at me with hate. PSALM 35:16

Marna, fresh from a treatment center for chemical dependency, knocked on the door of her former employer. As he greeted her warmly, her palms began to sweat, and her voice trembled. "I need to talk to you."

During her last days of treatment, she had been encouraged by her counselors to begin working on the Eighth Step, making a list of all the persons she had hurt. Her list was long, but her employer was near the top. She had stolen from the cash drawer, falsified her time card, and given her friends food. And when she quit, she had recommended a friend for the job and then taught the friend all her tricks.

She knew her employer had the right to be angry, the right to hate her. She had no defense. What she had done was clearly wrong. He was the victim. And yet as she laid herself open to him, she felt helpless and vulnerable, as if she were crippled. But she was doing what she needed to do for her own health.

May God give us the courage to face those whom we have hurt.

May 21

Teach me, God, what you want me to do, and lead me along a safe path, because I have many enemies.
PSALM 27:11

Before going to talk to her former employer, Marna had thought through what she could do to make amends for all that she had taken from him. She would offer to work without pay for a time, doing the best job she could. But she could not decide whether to tell him about the friend she had recommended to replace her, the friend who was also stealing from him.

Then she realized that the friend should also have been on her Eighth-Step list. She had hurt her friend by recommending her for the job and then teaching her how to steal.

Marna decided that it was her responsibility to explain to her employer how easy it was to steal from him and what he might do to prevent it. Then she went to her friend and apologized, telling her story of confession and making amends. From there on, it was out of her hands. Her Eighth Step in relationship to these two persons was as complete as she knew how to make it at the time.

May our God teach us what we should do to make amends.

May 22

Robbery always claims the life of the robber—this is what happens to anyone who lives by violence. PROVERBS 1:19

This verse comes at the end of a long admonition to young people to listen to their parents and stay away from anyone who might be a bad influence. There is an absoluteness about the warning that could work to frighten some young people into being good. But it could as easily produce cynicism among others as they see that people seem to get away with all kinds of wrongdoing without being punished.

Such cynicism can as easily be produced by any formula for leading a good life. "If you follow the Twelve Steps, you will achieve serenity." Or, "If you obey God and meditate daily, you will have a good life and peace of mind." This kind of thinking keeps our focus on the correctness of our behavior. Then, when we do everything we are supposed to do and our lives do not improve, we blame the formula or blame God. Such formulas are important and have their place, but a preoccupation with the right and wrong way to live stifles our spirituality, opening the door to cynicism and despair.

May our Deliverer free us to live beyond formulas and rules.

May 23

Never get a lazy person to do something for you; that person will be as irritating as vinegar on your teeth or smoke in your eyes. PROVERBS 10:26

The writer reflects a very common human situation. Whenever we try to get someone to do something for us that we ought to do for ourselves, whenever we attempt to use someone for our own purpose, we open ourselves up to being irritated or used. We also set up barriers in relationships and obstacles for our spiritual journey.

There is a good rule of thumb in child-rearing which applies to all relationships: Do not do for others what they can do for themselves. It is an equally good guideline turned around: Do not ask another to do something for you that you can do for yourself. This is particularly true regarding our emotional and spiritual lives. It is our responsibility to maintain our own disciplines, to keep our own inner house clean, and to foster positive relationships of our own. It is up to us to recognize when we truly need help and reach out for that help.

May the Source of our being help us grow toward maturity.

May 24

Your constant love is my guide; your faithfulness always leads me. PSALM 26:3

The farther they got from the base camp, the more the campers realized how dependent they were on their guide. Traveling through uninhabited wilderness territory with only canoes for transportation and a week's supply of food in their backpacks was frightening when they thought about their vulnerability. But it was exhilarating when they trusted the guide and lived each day to its fullest.

What does it mean to have God's love and faithfulness as our guide for our spiritual journey? Surely it has something to do with the way we love others and are faithful in our relationships. But, more important, it allows us to move into unexplored territory. It gives us the courage to take risks. It helps us move off the beaten path, to question the methods and standards of our culture or our religious group. Having a loving and faithful God as our guide is exhilarating and allows us to live each day to its fullest.

May we trust our faithful Guide this day.

May 25

When I was in trouble, you helped me. Be kind to me now and hear my prayer. PSALM 4:1B

It is both comforting and reassuring to reach a stage in our spiritual lives where we can look back and know that during a time of trouble God was present and did help. For those of us using the Twelve Steps both as a guide for living and as a guide for reflecting on our past lives, we recognize that this stage is the Eleventh Step. We have passed through times of great trouble and have let God take over. We have allowed God to work in our lives to give us a healthy self and healthy relationships. And we give credit to God as the one who provided those people and events to help us, and who gave us the insight and inner strength to persevere.

We are becoming people of prayer, people who daily seek God's will for our lives. We ask God to "be kind to [us] now" – not tomorrow or five years from now, but *now*. We set ourselves squarely in the day, recognizing its potential for nurturing our growth, its challenge for fostering our healing, and its opportunities for experiencing love.

May God show kindness to us today.

May 26

Then I looked again at all the injustice that goes on in this world. The oppressed were crying, and no one would help them. No one would help them, because their oppressors had power on their side. ECCLESIASTES 4:1

It was not that no one *could* help the oppressed, it was that no one *would*. And no one would help them because the power of the oppressor instilled fear in everyone. It takes no more than a glance at the front page of a newspaper to realize that oppression continues all over the world and that oppressors maintain their power in part, at least, because the rest of the world allows it. We stand back, afraid to get involved, afraid of getting hurt, convinced that it would be wasted effort anyway.

But the spiritual journey is a journey both inward and outward. We have discovered there is a power greater than ourselves, a power that has created—and continues to create—in us new and better ways of living. Because of this, we are also able to believe that that same power can and will work through us to challenge the powers of oppression in the world.

May our Creator's power flow through us to help heal a broken world.

May 27

There are many who pray, "Give us more blessings, O Lord. Look on us with kindness!" PSALM 4:6

The psalmist has observed that the prayers of many are prayers of request, asking God for more – more money, more things, more security. Perhaps the psalmist recalls a time in his own life when that was the way he prayed. But in the following verses the psalmist goes on to talk about the joy that God has given him, joy that is the best of all blessings.

The more we experience life, the more we realize that without certain spiritual qualities we repeatedly make problems for ourselves or make our existing problems worse. We are also unable to appreciate or use effectively the tangible blessings we receive. Nothing is ever enough.

And so we pray for peace of mind, for love, for self-control, for kindness, for generosity, for patience, for acceptance, for hope. These are the gifts that reflect God's own Spirit and that God most wants to shower on us.

May we be open to the richness of God's blessings.

May 28

Rescue me from death, O God, that I may stand before the people of Jerusalem and tell them all the things for which I praise you. PSALM 19:14

Sometimes it is easy to slip into thinking that the Twelve Steps for spiritual renewal are like rungs on a ladder, bringing us ever closer to perfection, ever nearer to God. But in reality they are more like steps in a path, leading us ever closer to others. By practicing these principles, we become persons who, little by little, are willing to share more genuinely, love more deeply, and serve more graciously. These Steps equip us to enter our worlds with humility, courage, and strength, thankful that God has rescued us from the death and darkness in which we were living, and trusting that God is also at work in the lives of others.

The Twelfth Step reflects not so much a conscious, deliberate action as it does the inevitable consequence of living the other Eleven Steps. When we have experienced a spiritual renewal, we *will* carry the message to others. By simply being who we are, we will speak through words and actions a message of hope.

May our lives tell of all that God has done for us.

May 29

Whenever you possibly can, do good to those who need it. PROVERBS 3:27

There is a story of a woman who would reach into her coin purse, take out money and put it in any parking meter she saw that had expired, thus saving the owner of the car from getting a ticket. She never knew whom she was helping and she knew they would never know it was she who had helped them. But she continued this practice until she was too old to walk the city streets any more.

According to a Jewish tradition, such acts are the second highest level of charity (the lowest level being the grudging gift after being asked, and the highest being gifts or ways of living that keep others from becoming impoverished or needy in the first place). As we engage in acts of kindness, it is important to clear out of our minds the expectation of gratitude or the hope that the receiver will think more highly of us because we gave. We grow toward the goal of generosity whenever we give because we have been given to, with no concern for the response of the other.

May our Highest Power bless us with giving hearts.

May 30

The more you talk, the more likely you are to say something foolish. ECCLESIASTES 5:3B

According to the writer, the underlying motivation for not talking so much is that we do not want to appear foolish in the eyes of others. Such self-interest may be a good way to get persons to slow down and talk less. But what we discover when we do talk less is that we listen more. We open ourselves up to hearing about the feelings and needs of others.

When we talk, our mental attention is on our ideas, our attitudes, our thoughts. When we really listen, we direct our attention away from ourselves and toward others. In the process, we worry less about ourselves, we concern ourselves less with what others are thinking about us, and we are less apt to get puffed up with our own self-importance. We are also able to learn much more about ourselves by learning about others. And when we listen, we are more able to cultivate the self-confidence of others, help them find their own solutions, and affirm who they are.

May our Helper develop in us the skill of listening.

May 31

They say to themselves, "I will never fail; I will never be in trouble." PSALM 10:6

It seems as if such words can hardly enter our minds or escape our lips before they are proved wrong. And yet, if we have been living in a time of spiritual serenity, it is easy to think we have arrived. We slide into thinking of spirituality as a state of being we can work toward and then reach because we deserve it.

It is silly to mar our good times by assuming that failure or trouble is just around the next corner. But there is a fine line between being superstitious about good times and becoming arrogant about them. When we become arrogant, we assume that we deserve all we have that is good and will continue to receive success and blessings because we are good.

Our Creator wants us to have problem-free times of peace. These times are gifts to us. As long as we receive them and treasure them as gifts, we will spare ourselves the problems and the aftermath of pride.

May our Creator protect us from arrogance and pride.

June

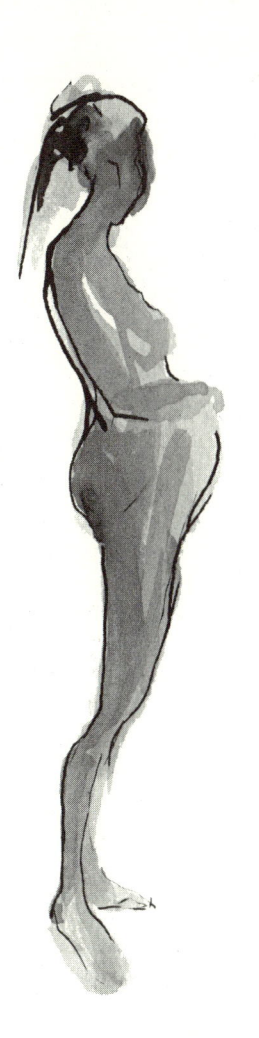

June 1

Better off than either are those who have never been born, who have never seen the injustice that goes on in this world. ECCLESIASTES 4:3

In Ecclesiastes 4:2, the verse just before this one, the writer refers to those who are already dead and those who still live, who still must deal every day with the frustrations of injustice. The writer says that it is better never to have been born at all than to have lived.

But, for us *that* is not an option. We were born. We do live. We do, however, have *some* options. We can choose what we want to see. Some of us seem, almost as if by instinct, to see only what is bad in life, to focus on the negative, to dwell on what is wrong. Others of us see only what is good, as if we had on blinders blocking out what we do not want to see.

Our goal is to keep a balance, to acknowledge what is bad both in ourselves and in our world and to do what we can to change it. But at the same time, we need to train our eyes to see beauty where it exists, love where it flows, kindness when it is offered.

May the Source of our lives give us clear vision and open hearts.

June 2

Whatever happens or can happen has already happened before. God makes the same thing happen again and again. ECCLESIASTES 3:15

The old expression, "Laugh and the world laughs with you, cry and you cry alone," has often been used to warn people that if they express sadness, they can expect to be deserted by others. And so, people keep their pain private, their fears bottled up inside, and they paste smiles on their faces for the world.

The saying likely originated as an observation, not an antidote to loneliness. When people are happy they want to be with others, but there is something about sadness, about pain, about failure that draws us in on ourselves. We assume others have never felt the way we feel, have never experienced what we are experiencing.

The life-giving reality is that there is nothing that has happened to us that has not happened to many others. There is nothing we can think or feel that has not been thought or felt before. Honesty with friends or in support groups can give us the help we need during difficult times.

May our Helper bless us with friends who understand our pain.

June 3

Lord, I call to you for help; every morning I pray to you. Why do you reject me, Lord? Why do you turn away from me? PSALM 88:13-14

During those times in life when we feel abandoned by God, when we call for help but it does not come, maybe we need to look at ourselves to see if there is something about us that needs to change before God can help us. Maybe it is our self-righteousness, our martyrdom, our insistence on having a plan of action, our refusal to accept our limitations, or our refusal to admit our strengths.

The First Step involves the process of determining which of our attitudes are counterproductive and block us from accepting God's help in our lives. We can begin by making a list of the points of great frustration in our lives and then acknowledging the futility of most of the ways we have chosen to deal with these frustrations. Looking over the list, we can admit our powerlessness.

May God lead us through the death of futile attitudes and habits and toward new life.

June 4

People who bring trouble on their families will have nothing in the end. PROVERBS 11:29

The biblical message is that families are important and that we are responsible to and for our family (those persons with whom we live and work most closely). People who deliberately attempt to hurt their families will bring suffering and emptiness on themselves.

A family is like a garden filled with a variety of flowers, each different, each valuable in its own way. We are at the same time both the gardener and part of the garden. As gardener, we plant and water, we cultivate and prune, we pluck weeds and spread mulch, and we rejoice in the growth and beauty of the garden.

As part of the garden, we recognize that we cannot grow by our own effort. We will shrivel up and die if we do not absorb the love we need, accept the criticism we receive, and treasure the help others in the family want to give.

May the Creator of all help us see ourselves as both gardener and part of the garden.

June 5

But I am poor and needy; O God, hasten to me! You are my help and my rescuer; O Lord, do not delay.
PSALM 70:5

To believe in a God, a Creator, a Higher Power, who is not involved in our daily lives is easy. We cannot be proven wrong. But to believe in a God who is active in our daily lives puts our faith on the line. Our own reasoning, our own experience, our own fears tell us that we are wrong over and over again. "If God is good and God is active in daily life, then . . . why? Why? Why?

The Second Step is a statement that flies in the face of evidence, that overrules reason, that is often hard to prove by our past experience.

But God understands our need for proof and wants to give us eyes that can see all of the ways in which God is at work in our lives. And so our Creator says to us, "You have learned that you are helpless in this particular area of your life. Give it to me and trust me. I want to show you how much I love you by giving you what you need."

Little by little God will give us both proof and eyes to see it.

May we be given eyes to see our Creator's work in our lives.

June 6

O Lord, don't stay away from me! Come quickly to my rescue. PSALM 22:19

The last phrase of the Third Step refers to God as understood by us. How we understand God depends in great measure on our past experiences. The psalmist understands God as one who rescues people in trouble. But that is not the only understanding of God. Some understand God as provider, as helper, as comforter, or as forgiver.

For those of us fortunate enough to have a positive image of God, the Third Step, "making a decision to turn our will and our lives over to the care of God," is much easier. But many have been taught that God is a judge who is eager to punish – an all-knowing Santa Claus who will leave switches and ashes in our stockings if we have not been good. It is difficult to trust such a God. Sometimes that teaching came through the image of God as a father coupled with our negative experiences with our own fathers. Finding new images of God, perhaps as a mother, as shelter, or as a counselor, can help us with the Third Step.

May we grow in our understanding of a gracious God.

June 7

You can be ruined by the talk of godless people, but the wisdom of the righteous can save you. PROVERBS 11:9

Over and over again, the Bible speaks of the incredible power of words, both to hurt and to heal, to take life and to give life, to choke relationships and to breathe life into them.

But in this verse the writer is talking, not about the words spoken between people in relationships, but about those impersonal words we take in daily. In our time they would be words read in newspapers, magazines, or books; words heard in discussions, on TV, or in movies. Not all such words are good for us. Some build up, but others ruin. Some uplift, others tear down.

We cannot live on a mountain top safe from any bad influence. Indeed we would not want to. But we need to remember that we are not immune from the kind of destruction some words can cause. Certain words may produce in us anger or hate, lust or other cravings, resentment or envy, self-pity or cynicism. Until we learn to control our responses, we should avoid those words. Knowing ourselves well enough to be our own censor is part of spiritual growth.

May our Protector give us wisdom to choose carefully what we read and listen to.

June 8

So I let them go their stubborn ways and do whatever they wanted. PSALM 81:12

It would seem from this verse that God was the originator of the concept of "tough love"—love that at some point lets go, hoping that the loved one will come to his or her senses outside of the orbit of family love, support, and discipline.

Those of us who have been the objects of tough love know how cold and alone it feels when suddenly we are, in fact, alone. We are without anyone to run defense for us, anyone to bail us out, anyone to blame for our difficulties but ourselves, anyone to put salve on our wounds. Life becomes very painful, and we remember what we had, what we forfeited through our own destructive behavior.

The success of tough love depends in large measure on the strength of good memories. Our Creator, like a good parent, gives and gives and gives, hoping that if it is ever necessary to let us go our stubborn ways, we will remember and return, ready once again to live and grow as a part of God's family.

May the Creator of all help us see the many good things we have been given.

June 9

Examine me and test me, Lord; judge my desires and thoughts. PSALM 26:2

If asked what we want most out of life, what are our likely answers? Success? Status? Economic security? A good reputation? A significant relationship? Children who do well? Good health? The list is endless.

One good way to approach the Fourth Step is to make a list of all of our desires, and then examine the list and note what patterns are evident. For instance, do our desires reflect an obsession with security, a need to have the future in hand, the inability to live one day at a time? Can we see a pattern that reflects a deep need to be respected or looked up to by others, an obsession with what others think, a refusal to keep our focus on ourselves? Perhaps our desires tell us that we want to be able to control those we love, to ensure that their lives are managed well, that they do what we think is right.

A careful examination of our desires can teach us much about ourselves. They point out those areas of our lives that we have not yet turned over to the care of God.

May God give us honesty and insight in our Fourth Step.

June 10

It is foolish to speak scornfully of others. If you are smart, you will keep quiet. PROVERBS 11:12

This proverb and the saying which is so like it, "If you haven't anything good to say about someone, don't say anything at all," are bits of wisdom designed to help protect us from one of our most basic impulses — seeing and talking about the faults of others.

One way we can constructively use that impulse is to make a list of those persons we have disliked most throughout our lives, then determine what specific traits in those persons we find so objectionable. As we go through the list, we will likely find a pattern, one which tells us something very important about ourselves. The traits we most dislike in others are often those parts of ourselves that we have never accepted, those weaknesses that we do not want to recognize or think about. If what we do not like in others is their intolerance, their phoniness, their two-facedness, their irresponsibility. . . , then we know where to begin in our own journey toward self-awareness.

May the Source of our being guide us in our efforts to understand ourselves.

June 11

He does no wrong to his friends and does not spread rumors about his neighbors. PSALM 15:3B

Neighbors are not necessarily our friends, nor are our friends necessarily our neighbors, but we have a responsibility to both. That responsibility is to live in as loving, honorable, and dependable a relationship as possible. The secret to such peaceful co-existence is to somehow separate our behavior from the behavior of the other.

When a neighbor behaves irresponsibly, that does not justify an angry, hurtful response from us. If a friend breaks a bond of trust, we are not given permission to respond in kind. How easy it is to fall into the trap of rationalizing our own behavior by noting the behavior of the other. "She started it!" "He made me do it!" "She deserves it!"

We have learned through the Twelve Steps that we cannot make another person do anything. Neither can someone else make us do anything. We choose our own behavior, and we are responsible for that choice and its consequences.

May God help us separate ourselves from the negative behavior of others and make good choices.

June 12

Then I confessed my sins to you; I did not conceal my wrongdoings. PSALM 32:5A

The psalmist is talking about confession to God and goes on to proclaim the assurance of God's forgiveness. But we have all likely had experiences with confession that have not gone so well. We have told someone of our sin, and that person has been shocked, angered, or disillusioned. We have admitted a wrongdoing to a family member, and that member has cut us off. We have confided in a friend, and that friend has prodded us out of curiosity and then betrayed our confidence. Confession can be risky business.

When we decide we are ready to do our Fifth Step, it is important to find a person who is absolutely trustworthy. This person should understand the Twelve-Step process, the purpose of a Fifth Step, and be experienced in communicating God's unconditional love and forgiveness. With such a person, a Fifth Step can be that occasion when, with confidence and openness, we pour out all the times and all the ways we have hurt others and ourselves.

May God bless us with trustworthy confessors.

June 13

Those who love knowledge want to be told when they are wrong. It is stupid to hate being corrected. PROVERBS 12:1

It may be unwise to hate being corrected, but still, being corrected is usually a painful experience and not always a welcomed one. Having to admit that we were wrong is bad enough when we have figured it out for ourselves, but being told by another compounds the pain.

We know how much such correction hurts. But sometimes, in relation to those with whom we live and work, we forget how painful it is. Thoughtlessly, we directly or indirectly point out their failings, their mistakes, their inferiority.

Sometimes we point out another's faults by boasting about ourselves or exclaiming about the success of another. Other times we lose our tempers in private or make pointed digs in public.

Whatever our tactic, if our correction of another is not grounded in deep love and respect, it will tear down both the other person and the relationship. Being able to accept correction is a sign of maturity. Being able to give it effectively is a sign of great maturity and compassion.

May our Helper give us the maturity to both accept and give correction.

June 14

Restore us, O God! Show us your favor that we may be delivered. PSALM 80:3

This verse reflects the psalmist's concern for the whole community – restore *us*. All of us are members of many groups. We are citizens of a nation, state, city. We live in a neighborhood. We usually live with one or more persons and may work closely with others. We belong to religious organizations, clubs, and small groups. Because groups can suffer from the same kinds of dis-ease as individuals, the Twelve Steps can be used to help groups recover.

From time to time, we need to look fearlessly at the strengths and weaknesses of our groups (Fourth Step), to admit the ways in which they are not functioning effectively (Fifth Step), and to do the Sixth Step – be ready to have God work on the relationships within the group and the spirit of the group in order to enhance its health and effectiveness. Any institution can be made healthier, and no community, however large or small, however dysfunctional, however split apart, is beyond the saving grace of God.

May God work to restore health to the groups of which we are a part.

June 15

Satisfy us at daybreak with your steadfast love that we may sing for joy all our days. PSALM 90:14

The human spirit abhors a vacuum. When we ask God, as a part of the Seventh Step, to remove our shortcomings, a vacuum is created. If we are not careful, a shortcoming as bad or worse than the one removed can creep in. We ask God to remove the bigotry or intolerance from ourselves or our communities, and before long we discover that we have swung to the other extreme. We accept everyone and anything. We have lost our values, our sense of moral outrage at real injustice, our ability to see evil where it exists. Or we ask God to break down the walls that separate us from those we love, and when our family's health is restored, we become filled with self-righteousness, judging others who are in the same position we once were.

Whether we are working on individual shortcomings or the problems of a group, we need to always follow a prayer for removal of something bad with a prayer for filling with something good. "Fill us each morning with your constant love...."

May our Highest Power replace our shortcomings with joy and love.

June 16

When fools are annoyed, they quickly let it be known. Smart people will ignore an insult. PROVERBS 12:16

Learning how to handle real or imagined insults is a major task for most of us in our spiritual journeys. Perhaps we have been ignored or left out. Maybe we have been publicly ridiculed or put down. Whatever the source, the most automatic response is to repay in kind – to return the insult, to turn our back on the individual, or to try to turn others against that person.

The writer of this proverb says that if we are smart, we will ignore an insult. That means that we disregard it, we do not respond to it. It is relatively easy to learn to control our behavior so that we do not respond externally to an insult. But controlling our feelings is quite another thing. We hold onto insults, letting them grow into resentments – resentments that eat away at us from the inside out. The process is insidious, the results deadly. Learning to truly ignore an insult is a gift from our Helper. Pray that God will help you grow in this life-giving ability.

May our Helper give us the wisdom to know how to ignore an insult.

June 17

How often they rebelled against God in the wilderness; how many times they made God sad! PSALM 78:40

The psalmist is talking about the Israelites as they wandered from slavery in Egypt to the Promised Land. It was necessary that they spend years in the wilderness learning to entrust their freedom to God. It was not an easy task, and they often failed.

How like those Israelites we are. God is leading us from the slavery of addictions of one kind or another, and God wants to bring us to the Promised Land. But the journey is filled with troubles we had not foreseen, problems that seem to have no solution. And so we become angry with God, demanding a solution. And, as the psalmist tells us, God responds with sadness.

Perhaps, as we work on our Eighth Step, God should be at the top of our list. In what ways have we, as individuals or as parts of a group, hurt God through our rebellion, our lack of trust, our shortsightedness, our worry? In what ways have we broken communication with our Creator? How have we made our Comforter sad?

May we sense God's personal involvement in our lives.

June 18

Then God led his people out like a shepherd and guided them through the wilderness. PSALM 78:52

God's greatest delight was in being able to do for the Israelites what a good shepherd can do best — lead, guide, and care for. Imagine the joy God feels when loved people, who have been brought out of slavery or pain of any kind, will trust and follow their Shepherd.

When we have refused to follow or ceased to trust, the only amend that God wants from us as a part of our Ninth Step is a return to faithfulness. For others we have hurt, we may have to do specific acts, repay in tangible ways. But God's love is so gracious that its only requirement, when we have rebelled and done things that have been hurtful, is that we return and let God, once again, guide our lives.

Over and over again the people of Israel wandered away from their shepherd and fell prey to their enemies. God never stopped loving them or trying to help them, and the Good Shepherd's joy when they returned is repeated every time one of us once again trusts God.

May we follow our Shepherd's leading through our wilderness times.

June 19

A good wife is her husband's pride and joy; but a wife who brings shame on her husband is like a cancer in his bones. PROVERBS 12:4

This verse brings into sharp focus the influence that our behavior has on the people in our families or those who are close to us. In a novel by Elie Wiesel, a young Israeli freedom fighter has been told that he must execute an English soldier. As he waits, unable to sleep, through the long night before the execution, he envisions his parents and grandparents with him along with his former teachers and friends. They are all there because what he is about to do reflects on them as well as on him. They do not tell him what to do, they just let him know that it matters. He is what is left on earth of them.

But our behavior not only reflects on those who influenced us, it also directly affects for better or for worse those we live with now. Behaving in ways that foster feelings of shame in our partner or children, parents or friends, employers or employees does to the spirit what cancer does to the body.

May the Source of our being give us wisdom and control over our own behavior.

June 20

God sets the time for finding and the time for losing, the time for saving and the time for throwing away.
ECCLESIASTES 3:6

Over and over, the Bible makes it clear that God is a God who is not only interested in our spiritual well-being but is also interested in our possessions, in the things with which we surround ourselves. Those of us who have moved after living for a time in a home know how many things we accumulate over the years and how important many of them are. There is the ceramic dog purchased at the drug store and given to us for Valentine's Day by our six-year-old. Or the souvenirs that remind us of wonderful vacations. Or the plaque noting an accomplishment or membership in a group.

There is a time for saving, for holding onto the things that have meaning because they connect us to the memory of a person, a place, or an event. But there comes a time when these things become a burden, when we need to break with the past in order to move on. And at those times, we need the strength and courage to throw away.

May our Helper give us the wisdom and courage to move forward.

June 21

God leads the humble in the right way and teaches them God's will. PSALM 25:9

There comes a point in our spiritual journeys when arrogance finds an easy opening and slides in almost undetected. That often happens after we have made amends to those we have hurt. We have worked very hard to understand ourselves and to let God remove our character defects. We have also taken seriously the task of making amends. We have, in fact, made great strides toward a healthy, whole life.

It is easy at this point to forget that we never could have done it without God's abundant help and mercy working within us and through others. It is also a temptation to judge others and blame those who are not as healthy as we are, perhaps suggesting to them exactly the path they should follow to become healthier.

Such arrogance or self-righteousness is a serious defect of character. By working the Tenth Step we can look at ourselves each day, check for places where arrogance is creeping in, and humbly admit the problem, asking God to help us.

May God keep our hearts humble.

June 22

You do yourself a favor when you are kind. If you are cruel, you only hurt yourself. PROVERBS 11:17

The writer of this proverb is appealing to a vested self-interest in people. We do not want to hurt ourselves. So, if we think being cruel to another *will* hurt us, we will be more careful, more kind. Those of us who have raised children know there are some children for whom this is the only motivation that seems to work.

Adults are no different. Some of us are so immune to the feelings of others that the only thing that stops us from saying or doing whatever we feel is the fear that we, ourselves, will pay a price if we are cruel.

This fear can be positive if it works to control our behavior. But at the same time we need to ask God to help us grow in our ability to be kind for the sake of the other, to be loving simply because we are loved by God, to be generous with no thought of return. In other words, we need to ask God's help in doing to others what we would like to have them do to us, rather than not doing harm to others so that they will not hurt us.

May God fill us with love and concern for others.

June 23

The wise get all the knowledge they can, but when fools speak, trouble is not far off. PROVERBS 10:14

Persons who want to get involved in the political system or some social action project are well advised to learn everything there is to know about the system or cause before speaking out. If their comments indicate ignorance, they will be disregarded, no matter how valid their point.

Knowledge neither guarantees wisdom or truth nor prevents us from making mistakes. Knowledge must continually be held up for scrutiny. But choosing to remain uninformed, whether in personal matters or on social issues, leads inevitably to foolish decisions. We live in a time when the amount of available information about virtually anything is overwhelming. One hardly knows where to begin. And yet we are challenged to decide which concerns are priorities for us and then begin learning what there is to know.

God also has provided abundant resources to help us learn about divine providence, divine love, divine goodness. God wants us to know all we can know for our spiritual journeys.

May the Source of all wisdom nurture in us the desire for knowledge.

June 24

You give me strength for the battle and victory over my enemies. PSALM 18:39

What does it mean to know God's will for us, which is the prayer of the Eleventh Step? God makes no secret about what that will is—it is that we be connected to God, be reliant on God. And God is love.

So, what does that mean for us as we attempt to work the Eleventh Step? Each day we face enemies both within and without, enemies that try to make us appreciate less and fear more, trust less and worry more, accept less and judge more. Love is the most powerful antidote to fear, dispeller of worry, and cure for judgmentalism. And God is love.

The strength we receive for our battles against our enemies both within and without comes from a strange weapon—the weapon of vulnerability, of honesty, of caring, of tolerance, of love. And God is love.

It is God's will that we rid ourselves of our angers, our fears, our compulsions to criticize, our attempts to control—that we rid ourselves of these and replace them with love. And God will help us for God is love.

May the God of love fill us with love for ourselves and others.

June 25

God has given us a desire to know the future, but never gives us the satisfaction of fully understanding what God does. ECCLESIASTES 3:11

The writer of Ecclesiastes reflects a frustration that seems to be common to all persons attempting to relate to God and walk a spiritual path. We want to do the right thing, make the right decision, act in the most loving way. But the only way to know what that right decision is would be to know the future, to know just how our actions will affect us and others. The more serious we are about making good choices, the more we try to guess or predict what the impact of those choices will be.

But the reality of life, and the frustration, is that we can never fully know the impact of our choices even after the fact. Neither can we ever know how our actions, our choices, even our mistakes, are used to work God's purposes. That is why we are told to keep our focus on the day. Our only responsibility is to live as authentically and honestly and lovingly as we can today. Our future and the futures of those we love are in good hands.

May God help us keep our focus on the day.

June 26

How can anyone be sure that a human's spirit goes upward while an animal's spirit goes down into the ground? ECCLESIASTES 3:21

How can we know? How can we be sure? How can we dare to risk putting our lives in the hands of God when we have no real proof that those hands are even there or that they will hold us and guide us.

The honest answer is that we cannot know for sure. We cannot prove the existence of God. We cannot demonstrate conclusively that God is active in our lives. Many spend their whole lives saying, "I would believe in God if only I could see some proof."

The reality of the spiritual journey is that we must start walking and keep walking without that proof. Even though we are not sure, we must base our lives on the assumption that there is a caring God. As we step out in trust, acting on the belief that there is a caring God, proof comes to us individually, little by little. And before long, we do know for sure.

May our journeys be blessed with proof of God's love.

June 27

Be generous, and you will be prosperous. Help others, and you will be helped. PROVERBS 11:25

The order of these simple sentences is of utmost importance. The writer does not say, "If you want to be prosperous, be generous. If you want to be helped, help others." Rather the writer is observing that people who are generous with themselves and with their possessions, people who see themselves as a part of a flow of love rather than a repository for love, those people receive in the same way that they give.

There is no way to know for sure that if you give you will receive. And that is a good thing. For, if there were proof, it would be almost impossible to keep our motivations other-centered. We would give so that we would be given to, help so that we would be helped.

As it is, we are asked to act out of faith, to give with no thought of the return. But those who allow themselves to become a part of the flow of possessions, assistance, and love observe that no matter how much they give, they are always filled.

May the Creator of all give us faith so that we can give generously.

June 28

In the full assembly I will praise you for what you have done. PSALM 22:25A

The common notion of our society is that we take in order to have and that to give is somehow to have less. Twelve-Step living involves the process of taking all of our common notions, all of the assumptions that we have believed without ever really questioning them, and turning them upside down and inside out.

What we discover is that when we take from another in order to have, we not only have less, we become less. And when we give to another for the sake of the other, we not only have more, we become more. It makes no sense. It is impossible to understand unless we have lived it. But countless people involved in spiritual living can attest to its truth.

In fact, the Twelfth Step – carrying the message to others – is all about the kind of giving that fills us up. Our spiritual lives become like a pool of stagnant water unless we cut channels connecting us to others and let love and caring flow freely.

May the Source of life fill us with love overflowing.

June 29

People who are proud will soon be disgraced. It is wiser to be modest. PROVERBS 11:2

There is a difference between being proud and having pride. People who are proud set themselves up, look down on others, and behave in ways that attempt to make others feel inferior. The need to be seen as superior is usually rooted in deep feelings of inferiority. When we find ourselves wanting to put others down, wanting to be seen as important, wanting to have power or influence over others, we can always see that as a sign of spiritual dis-ease. For some reason we are neither accepting nor feeling good about ourselves. When we detect in ourselves the symptoms of arrogance, we must take it as a serious sign of spiritual dis-ease, dis-ease needing the healing power of God.

People who have pride in themselves, love themselves, and accept themselves as God's handiwork have no need to act arrogant. They have no need to control others, lord it over others, or put others down.

Our goal is to overcome arrogance by nurturing God-centered pride in ourselves.

May God fill us with good feelings about ourselves.

June 30

They spoke against God and said, "Can God supply food in the wilderness?" PSALM 78:19

The reassuring message of the story of the journey of the people of Israel through the wilderness is that God came to their aid and provided the people with food – even when they grumbled and complained, even when they spoke against God, even when they had no faith that God could or would help them.

We, too, are God's chosen people. We, too, are traveling through what often seems like a wilderness, a place where it is very difficult to satisfy even our most basic needs. We, too, often grumble and complain and doubt that God can help us in any meaningful way.

But even as God sent manna from heaven – wafers of bread to satisfy the hunger of the Israelites each day – so God sends to us, each day, what we need for that day. Maybe it is as simple as a phone call from an old friend or a letter from a child. Maybe it is a smile or kind word from a stranger. It could be a task to fill our time and stretch our minds. Whatever it is, God is at work each day giving us what we need for the day.

May we have eyes to see the gracious hand of God in our lives.

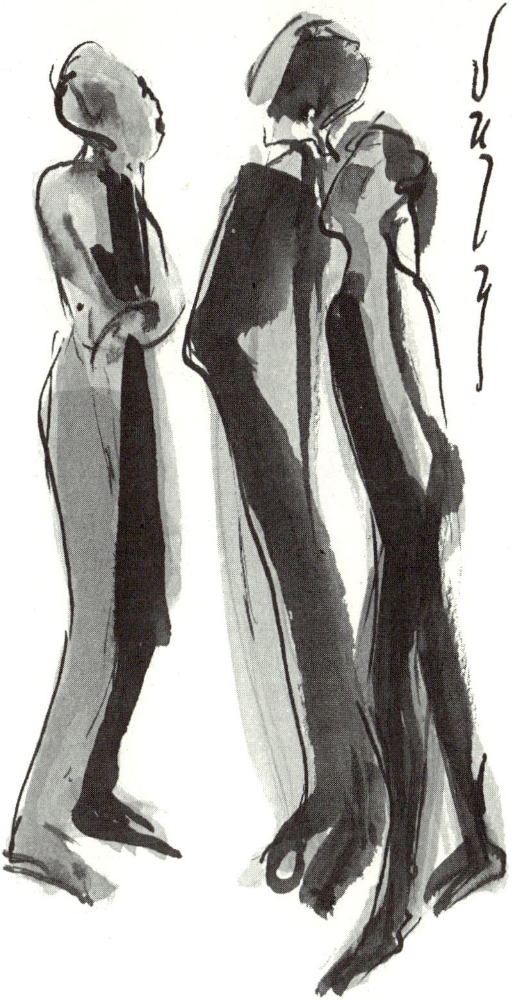
July

July 1

It is better to be an ordinary person working for a living than to play the part of a great person but go hungry. PROVERBS 12:9

We live in a society obsessed with being #1. We live among people equally obsessed with their own version of being the best. One must be great to be noticed, at the top to be recognized as having worth.

However, the reality of life is that very few people are ever the best at anything, and no one stays there for long. All of us, most of our lives, are less than best. In fact, we are more ordinary than we like to admit. Because it is hard to admit that we are ordinary, we sometimes pretend, play-act, and treat others as if we are better than they. In so doing, we set up barriers between ourselves and others. These barriers prevent us from being fed by others the love, kindness, and affirmation we need for growth. And so we go hungry.

It is better to admit that we are ordinary and humbly connect ourselves with the rest of humanity, recognizing our similarities rather than striving for superiority.

May the Creator of all give us joy in our ordinariness.

July 2

Arrogance causes nothing but trouble. It is wiser to ask for advice. PROVERBS 13:10

Arrogance comes in many disguises. Sometimes arrogance is the belief that we know what is best for ourselves. Or, it can be the assumption that we truly understand others and can judge their behavior or tell them what they need. Arrogance often masks itself as strong faith—we know the truth and do not need to listen, question, or struggle anymore.

At its root, arrogance is a replacement of God with self. We want to control ourselves and our futures. We want to know that we are right. We want to have the power over others that comes from thinking we can know what is best for them.

Such arrogance sets us up as competitors with both God and others. We vie for control, we struggle for power. Such a perspective "causes nothing but trouble,"—trouble between ourselves and God and trouble between ourselves and others. But the trouble diminishes when we step back, admit we do not always know what is best, and humbly ask for advice and help.

May God give us humble hearts.

July 3

O yes, I know what they say: "If you have reverence for God, everything will be all right, but. . . ." ECCLESIASTES 8:12

The writer of Ecclesiastes goes on to point out the abundant evidence of times when all has not been right for God's people, of times when bad things have happened to those who are good. We are caught in the tension between our belief that God is active in our lives, supporting and protecting us, and our observation that bad things do happen, things that have no reason or explanation.

We search for an answer to the question of why the innocent suffer. But we discover, as we struggle along on our spiritual journey, that we can be sure of only one thing: if we do come up with an answer, sooner or later something will happen to prove our answer wrong.

Then we are left, once again, with the question. But, more important, we are left with a very special relationship to our Creator—a creator who encourages our questions and helps us live courageously without answers.

May our Creator help us as we struggle with our questions.

July 4

Yes, I was great, greater than anyone else who had ever lived in Jerusalem, and my wisdom never failed me. . . . And I realized that it didn't mean a thing.
ECCLESIASTES 2:9, 11

Anyone living in Jerusalem at the time that this writer lived would have known and respected him. He would have been one of those persons we see as "having it all," as "having made it." How we envy such people. We assume that their self-image matches our image of them, that the outer symbols of success have given them confidence, peace, and happiness. But such is not usually the case.

When we are at the low ebbs of our days, those times when we are faced with our own powerlessness and the unmanageability of our lives, the risk of succumbing to envy or jealousy is particularly great. We need to remind ourselves of the First Step, which says, *"we* are powerless," *"our* lives have become unmanageable." We are not alone. In fact, all humanity struggles with the same problems in one way or another. We can feel a bond even with those who seem to have it all.

May the Source of all help us recognize the bonds that connect us to others.

July 5

O let none who look to you be disappointed; let the faithless be disappointed, empty-handed. PSALM 25:3

The psalmist likely thought of the world as divided into two camps—those who look to God and those who are faithless. But an honest look at ourselves makes us aware that we are also divided. There are parts of ourselves that we trust to God's care and other parts that we hold onto, telling God that we do not want or need any help. We can do it ourselves. This act of holding on is the insanity implied in the Second Step.

It was crazy, she knew it, but every time she was upset over something at work, she came home and ate, and ate, and ate. It took her weeks to lose a few pounds, and in one night she could negate all her efforts. Even while she was doing it, she thought about how angry she was going to be with herself the next morning when she stepped on the scale, but still she ate.

When introduced to the Twelve Steps, she knew immediately what the First and Second Steps were all about. It was insane the way she ate, and she was powerless to stop.

May we trust the power of our Maker in our areas of powerlessness.

July 6

This is all that I have learned: God made us plain and simple, but we have made ourselves very complicated. ECCLESIASTES 7:29

We wonder what it would be like to live as "plain and simple" people without all of the complications that have resulted from our childhoods and our own poor choices. Many of those complications make it hard for us to love ourselves and to love others. They prevent us from living free and open lives. They lead us into being dishonest with both ourselves and others.

One of the Twelve-Step slogans is "keep it simple." It reminds us of our tendency to make things more complicated than they need to be. It sets as our goal the kind of simplicity that God intended for us.

If one of the ways we tend to complicate our lives is by analyzing and then trying to fix the people with whom we associate most closely, we need to remind ourselves to "keep it simple." Our only responsibility is to love them. If we make our lives complicated by trying to be seen as something we are not, we need to "keep it simple" —be ourselves.

May God help us overcome unnecessary complications in our lives.

July 7

When hope is crushed, the heart is crushed, but a wish come true fills you with joy. PROVERBS 13:12

One of the most frightening things that can happen to us is the loss of hope, particularly the loss of hope that our lives will ever be any better. We feel empty, sapped of strength, depleted of energy. It is hard to think of any reason to keep trying. Indeed, our hearts are crushed.

Often our loss of hope is a realistic, rational, sane response to the events of our lives. At these times we need to believe that a power greater than ourselves can lift us above the rational into a spiritual arena where we can transcend reason, and over-ride reality. We need to believe that God can help us find hope, when there is no tangible reason to hope, and trust, when there is no obvious reason to trust.

During those times when we feel as if our hearts are crushed and there is no reason to expect that our wishes will ever come true, our prayer can be simply, "God, give me hope – hope based on the knowledge that you want what is best for me."

May our Comforter give us the precious gift of hope.

July 8

In my trouble I called to the Lord; I called to my God for help. . . . God heard my voice and listened to my cry for help. PSALM 18:6

The Third Step involves a decision to turn our wills and our lives over to God. Often our initial Third-Step decision is made during a time of great trouble, a time when we have used up all of our own resources and have no other options—something akin to a "fox-hole conversion."

As our lives become less troubled, it is easy to begin, little by little, to take back our wills, to reclaim parts of our lives. We like the feeling of being in control, of figuring out what we need, of making our own decisions. So our spiritual journey ends up being a cycle of turning our lives over to the Source of all life and then taking them back, over and over again.

The Third Step is one we need to renew every morning. "Just for today, God, I will turn my will and my life over to you, and for twenty-four hours I will try not to take it back." What we could not accomplish once and for all, we can accomplish one day at a time.

May the Source of life help us in our daily decisions.

July 9

My father and mother may abandon me, but the Lord will take care of me. PSALM 27:10

To be abandoned by one's parents either emotionally or physically is a traumatic experience no matter what age we are. Such abandonment can happen through illness or death, divorce or separation, or any of the addictions that make our parents incapable of loving us. We feel deserted and forsaken, as if the solid ground we were walking on had suddenly turned to swamp.

For some of us, this is the point when we can begin to know and experience God's care. As long as we have loving parents to support us, we do not need God in the same way. We lean on our parents and go to them for advice, nurturing, and love. Our Creator is using our parents to support us, but it is hard for us to feel those creative hands as long as the hands of our parents are holding us.

To be abandoned by our parents, painful as that is, can be the experience that draws us into an intimate relationship with God.

May we experience the direct care of our Creator in our lives.

July 10

Those who depend on their wealth will fall like the leaves of autumn, but the righteous will prosper like the leaves of summer. PROVERBS 11:28

In many ways, the leaves of autumn are more beautiful than the leaves of summer—they are multicolored and vibrant, catching the eye, filling the senses. People who conspicuously use their wealth (or perhaps their status, power, intellect, or personality) affect us the same way. We like to look at them. We admire their "color," envy their life.

The real danger is that our envy of these people will alter our relationship to God. Without a strong "God connection," we begin to take on the traits of these others. We learn to play the game by their rules, assuming that then we, too, will be admired.

But the leaves of autumn have lost their lifeblood; they will fall with the slightest wind. So it is with those who depend on anything but the Source of all life. When we are connected to God, we remain alive, soaking up the nourishment needed to live creatively.

May the Source of life keep us alive and green as the leaves of summer.

July 11

When I did not confess my sins, I was worn out from crying all day long. PSALM 32:3

As we work on the moral inventory suggested by the Fourth Step, it is, in some ways, good to remain as objective as one would while taking an inventory of a store—"I have five of this and eight of that." But there is a danger in being too objective, of not placing a moral value on the traits we discover in ourselves. For instance, we might say of ourselves, "I am the kind of person who holds grudges," or "I am a person who judges others," as if these were neutral traits.

There is no chance that our lives will ever become better unless we take a moral inventory and discover what we are. But we need to go one step further and label the character traits we discover for what they are—traits that help us live free, loving, God-centered lives or traits that work against us in obvious or subtle ways. We must claim our own responsibility for what is wrong. "Yes, I am guilty. I lie, express anger, lust, resent, judge, criticize, hurt, steal, hate. I can't blame anyone else. I am guilty."

May God give us the courage to see ourselves as we are.

July 12

Don't pay attention to everything people say . . . you know yourself that you have insulted other people many times. ECCLESIASTES 7:21–22

"Do you like everyone?" the counselor asked her after hearing her work-related story. "No, of course not," she responded. "Then why would you expect everyone to like you?" And then he asked her another question, "Do you always speak only kind words about others?" Of course, she knew that she often spoke unkind words about others but immediately began to justify herself. Her observations were, after all, true. Her criticism was, after all, needed. Her judgment was, after all, for their own good.

When she was all through talking, the counselor just sat and looked at her with raised eyebrows. Suddenly she heard herself. For the first time she realized that she was the source of the negativity in her relationships. The door of criticism is one that swings both ways. A forceful push out will almost guarantee an equally strong swing back in. We get back what we give.

May our Protector keep us from walking through the door of criticism.

July 13

Worry can rob you of happiness, but kind words will cheer you up. PROVERBS 12:25

When reading this verse, we assume that the kind words referred to are those spoken to us by others. If we are down, it is the responsibility of someone else to speak kindly to us to cheer us up.

But the writer of this proverb was balancing two activities that are within our control—worry and speaking kind words. We can choose whether to worry or not, and if we choose to worry, it will rob us of happiness. We can also choose whether to speak kind words or not, and if we do speak them, we will feel better. The first activity—worry—draws us in on ourselves and away from a trusting relationship with God. The second activity—speaking kind words—pulls us out of ourselves and forces us to observe others, feel what they may need, enter into the flow of love from one person to another, and speak words filled with graciousness.

One activity drains life out of us, the other pours life in. And we can choose which one we want to engage in.

May God fill us with kind words for others.

July 14

I have been evil from the time I was born; from the day of my birth I have been sinful. PSALM 51:5

The psalmist sounds like many people who have grown up in shame-based homes where every mistake provoked a label: "You're stupid," "You're clumsy," "You're irresponsible," "You're bad." When we have grown up with these labels, we cease to look at the things we have done as mistakes – mistakes for which we can ask forgiveness and make amends. Rather, we look at the bad things we do as the logical outgrowth of ourselves because we are bad.

There is a difference between the biblical message that each of us has within us a force that works against our well-being and the attitude that we are incompetent, irresponsible, unloveable, unredeemable, or evil from birth and to the core.

An effective Fifth Step will help us sort out legitimate guilt – the normal reaction to having made a mistake, to having hurt ourselves or others – and shame, that irrational sense of guilt for simply being.

May our Deliverer free us from any feelings of shame.

July 15

Save me from sinking in the mud; keep me safe from my enemies, safe from the deep water. PSALM 69:14

Much of our addictive or compulsive behavior stems from our feelings of shame. Living in shame is like sinking in mud. We flail about with our compulsive behaviors in an effort to pull ourselves out, to get on solid ground, but all we do is sink deeper and deeper.

We have admitted our powerlessness over the behavior. Now, we need to take a hard look at what is beneath the behavior. If we cannot seem to accept the love and forgiveness of others, if we know in our heads but not in our hearts that God forgives us, if we have trouble forgiving ourselves, then we are likely dealing with the problem of shame.

Shame, that sense of being absolutely unworthy, can be removed only with God's help. But we have to be ready. So we pray for God to implant in us the desire to have our feet on firm ground, to see ourselves as competent and loveable, and to walk the path of a responsible adult.

May God lift us out of the mud of shame and onto firm ground.

July 16

No one who gossips can be trusted with a secret, but you can put confidence in someone who is trustworthy. PROVERBS 11:13

The tendency to gossip, to delight in passing on private information about another person, is a character defect common to many of us. It is also a defect that is easily hidden beneath the mask of concern, love, or understanding.

Clearly, not all passing on of information about another is destructive. Sometimes it is important and necessary. But often our motivation for doing so does not spring from a deep concern for the well-being of the other.

We gossip because gossiping puts us in a position of power, both over the person about whom we are talking and the person to whom we are giving the information. It sets us apart as someone who knows. It gives us control and allows us to manipulate. But at the same time, it also takes us out of the flow of love, thus hurting both ourselves and the others involved.

Gossiping is a symptom of a defect of character we must be ready to have God remove: the desire for power over others.

May God free us from the desire to gossip.

July 17

May the Lord show his constant love during the day, so that I may have a song at night, a prayer to the God of my life. PSALM 42:8

When we have humbly asked God to remove our shortcomings (the Seventh Step), our next task is to be open to the ways in which God speaks to us. God's voice comes to us through our reading of the Bible and other spiritual writings. It also can come to us in the quiet of our meditations as a fragile thought or gentle nudge.

But often God uses the voices and behavior of those around us—sometimes even those we do not like—to help us see with honesty and clarity what we are doing or saying. When we find ourselves angered or hurt by the words or behavior of another, those feelings are a red flag telling us to stop, look at ourselves and ask, "What is God trying to tell me through this person and my response?" The things that anger us tell us much more about our points of spiritual dis-ease than almost anything else.

God works in our lives through many "voices."

May God make us ready to hear.

July 18

Beauty . . . without good judgment is like a gold ring in a pig's snout. PROVERBS 11:22

To understand the impact of this verse, we must realize that it was addressed to people who lived in a culture where pigs were seen as unclean animals. The writer is warning them not to be attracted by what is superficial, what is only skin deep, or they may be seduced into doing something that will make them unclean (touching a pig to get the gold ring).

There are many other ways this verse could be written to speak to our weaknesses: power in a person without compassion, charm in a person without love, intelligence in a person without humility, religion in a person without spirituality, wit in a person without hope. . . . What is it in other people that attracts us? Why? Are those qualities ones that will help to build us up or tear us down? Can we see beneath the surface, or are we caught by appearances? Honestly looking at the qualities in others that attract us can tell us much about ourselves and our need for replacing old values with new ones.

May God help us see beneath the surface.

July 19

You stopped being angry with them and held back your furious rage. PSALM 85:3

For years her father had abused her both emotionally and physically. During the process of doing her Fourth Step, the woman realized that her resentment toward her father had poisoned both herself and their relationship. She had struggled to forgive him and to get rid of the resentment, and she thought she had succeeded.

But as she worked on her Eighth-Step list of those she had hurt, she found herself thinking, "Wait a minute, he's the one that ought to be making amends to me." Or, "By making amends to him first, I will be showing him how much better a person I am than he."

Either thought process showed that she was not ready to make amends. She had not truly forgiven him, nor had she given up her resentment and need to get even.

As we prepare ourselves for making amends, we sometimes realize that we need to go back to the Fourth Step, recognizing and taking responsibility for a weakness, and then work through the next three steps before we can go on.

May our Helper prepare our hearts for making amends to those whom we have hurt.

July 20

Wicked people are trapped by their own words, but honest people get themselves out of trouble. PROVERBS 12:13

This proverb certainly speaks a truth about our relationships with others. As the familiar verse puts it, "Oh what a tangled web we weave, when first we practice to deceive." Dishonesty with others creates a sticky web from which only honesty can release us.

And the words apply equally to our relationship with ourselves. Rationalizing is one way we lie to ourselves; denying is another. Or we may honestly acknowledge a shortcoming but, through minimizing or exaggerating, distort it so that we can either ignore it or assume we can never overcome it. Our unhealthy self can find a thousand ways to keep us trapped in the web of dishonesty.

The ability to be honest with ourselves is a gift from God, a gift God is delighted to give to anyone who deeply wants it. Because each step in our spiritual journey requires honesty, this is a gift we can and should pray for daily.

May God give us the gift of honesty.

July 21

God heals the brokenhearted and bandages their wounds. PSALM 147:3

As we set to work on the Ninth Step – making direct amends to those we have hurt – it is so easy to slide into thinking we can heal the wounds we have caused. A mother, for instance, might have hurt her children by ignoring them, by attempting to turn them into puppets, by trying to turn them against their father, by unleashing bursts of temper, or by behaving in any manner that is hurtful to children. As she sets about making amends, it is important for her to remember that she cannot fix her children, she cannot heal the wounds she has caused, she cannot erase the impact of the negative words she has spoken. Only God can do that. Only God can heal their wounds.

With the freedom of knowing that their lives are not in her hands, the mother can set about making amends, giving them the attention and nurturing they now need, seeing in all the members of the family what is good, filling their minds with words of affirmation and praise, and respecting them enough to let them walk their own journeys.

May we trust the Healer of all with the lives of those we love.

July 22

Sensible persons gather the crops when they are ready; it is a disgrace to sleep through the time of harvest. PROVERBS 10:5

The image of crops and harvest is used often in the Bible. It meant a great deal to persons whose lives depended on growing their own food. If they slept through the harvest, they would lose the chance to feed themselves and their families.

The image has to do with observation and timing, and it speaks directly to those of us working to make amends to those whom we have hurt. For an amend to work toward healing, it must be done when the time is right—right for us and right for the other. If our amends are only for ourselves, if their purpose is only to relieve our guilt or help us feel better about ourselves, then they will likely backfire. Those we love will feel, once again, manipulated and used.

Our goal is to be so sensitive to the other that we will know when that person is ready. Then our amends can be a part of the other's growth.

May God give us sensitivity regarding the needs of others.

July 23

Help us, O God, and save us; rescue us and forgive our sins. PSALM 79:9

In order to pray with the psalmist, "Forgive our sins," we need to be conscious of our sin. A part of the Tenth Step is looking at ourselves, seeing what is wrong, and admitting it. This can be done many times during the day as a kind of spot check. The best way to do this is to note our danger signals: worrying, becoming envious, angry, or judgmental, losing energy, allowing ourselves to be victimized. Any of these problems points to an underlying spiritual problem.

Also, it is good to spend time at the end of each day taking an inventory of all our attitudes and behaviors of the day, feeling good about what we have done well and, again, confessing and turning over to God those times when we have failed.

It is also valuable, periodically, to look back over several months or even a year and assess where we have grown. In addition, we can openly note old problems that persist and new ones that have cropped up, confessing them and letting God wash us clean.

May we experience the wonder of God's forgiveness.

July 24

Obey God. . . . If you do, it will be like good medicine, healing your wounds and easing your pains. PROVERBS 3:8

How we long for the "good medicine" that will heal our wounds and ease our pains. But what does it mean to obey God? All religions have set about answering that question for their followers. What has resulted is that no matter which way we turn, we encounter a list of rules – some obvious, some covert – that we are to obey in order to be acceptable. Some groups stress private morality, others public deeds. Some emphasize spiritual experience, others religious commitment. Obedience is a many-faceted false gem.

The word "obey" has come to mean following a set of rules, but its original meaning was "to listen to." How different the verse becomes. "Listen to God" – be in relationship, be open to, care about. All the rules, like a ten-ton weight on our backs, can be set aside. God's healing power comes to us, not as a result of our good behavior or our careful adherence to all the rules, but through the relationship God has established with us.

May our Healer pour good medicine into our lives.

July 25

Never tell your neighbors to wait until tomorrow if you can help them now. PROVERBS 3:28

God's voice comes to us over and over again as we read the Bible, telling us that we cannot let our spirituality veer off into mysticism where all that is important is our relationship to God. The writers of all of the books of the Bible, but particularly Proverbs, keep in front of us the importance of the day to day relationships we have with those around us. Somehow our spiritual journey is intimately and integrally tied to our sister, our brother, our partner, our child, our parents, our friends, our employer or employee, our co-worker, our neighbor.

If we have the time or the emotional strength or the physical resources to help another, then it is our responsibility to do so. Putting off such acts of kindness until tomorrow, if we can do them today, suggests that these acts are unimportant to us and that we do not give high priority to others. It indicates that we have failed to see God in those around us.

May God help us to reach out lovingly to those in need.

July 26

I pray to you, O God, because you answer me; so turn to me and listen to my words. PSALM 17:6

Prayer (speaking to God) and meditation (listening to God) are the essence of the Eleventh Step. There is a wonderful dialogue involved, a dialogue between lovers. The Source of our lives wants us to talk, telling all of our problems and pains, all of our fears and anxieties, all of our hopes and joys. God is never bored with the details of our lives or too busy to tend to the little things that sometimes seem so big.

And God wants to respond, convincing us that we are loved, promising us that we are forgiven, assuring us that we are accepted just as we are. Our Creator wants to whisper to our hearts images of direction and words of hope. God wants to caress us tenderly, lifting us up when we are down, healing our wounds when we are hurt, correcting us when we are wrong, forgiving us when we are plagued with guilt, energizing us when we are ready to move out of ourselves and into the world. And, most important, God is always there loving us and waiting for us.

May we continue to seek God through prayer and meditation.

July 27

I say to the Lord, "You are my Lord; all the good things I have come from you." PSALM 16:2

The psalmist describes that stage in our spiritual journey when we have quit blaming God for the bad things in our lives, have stopped focusing our prayers on all that we want changed, and have developed eyes that see all that is good around us and within us. Not only do we see what is good, but we acknowledge it as a gift from our Creator who loves us.

For many of us, it takes a conscious effort to train ourselves to see what is good. Spend some time today and each day concentrating on something good about yourself, your life, your closest relationships, your job, your friends, your neighbors, your city and country—whatever people or institutions affect your life. Try to erase from your mind any if onlys, buts, or excepts. Think only of what is good.

Then think about your God, a God who wants to give you these good things and many more. Let your heart overflow with gratitude and love for your Creator.

May the Source of all good make us aware of that goodness.

July 28

The Lord is my light and my help; I will fear no one.
PSALM 27:1A

Asking the question "What is my greatest fear?" can tell us much about ourselves. Perhaps we fear ill health, divorce, death or loss of a loved one, public disgrace, job or career setbacks, war, poverty, loss of purpose in life. The list of possibilities is endless. Our observation tells us that there is much to fear in this world. Bad things do happen. People do get hurt in a thousand different ways.

Most of our fears result from envisioning people hurting us or bad things happening to us over which we have no control. We know, if we think about it, that spending our energy in fear is not going to prevent any of these things from happening. We also know that the degree of fear we have in our hearts is an indication of how much we have learned or not learned about trusting God as our "light and our help."

The Serenity Prayer, "God, help me to accept those things I cannot change. . . ," is a good antidote to fear.

May God help us fear less and trust more.

July 29

Save your people, Lord, and bless those who are yours. Be their shepherd, and take care of them forever. PSALM 28:9

Sometimes it is easy to forget that we are a part of a very large flock with a shepherd who is watching over the whole flock, guiding it, protecting it, leading it to good food and fresh water. Our shepherd is always on the lookout for any member of the flock who wanders off, always ready to search for, rescue, and return the lost one.

We are not the shepherd. We are not responsible for the whole flock. Nor are we responsible for any member of it except ourselves. We do not need to know the overall plan or the destination or how long it will take to get there. Neither do we need to know exactly how the shepherd is working in our lives or in the lives of other members of the flock.

We only need to be what we are: one member of a large flock, cared for and watched over by an absolutely trustworthy shepherd. We only need to know that our shepherd rescues, blesses, and cares for us forever.

May we follow the leading of our Shepherd.

July 30

The needy will not always be neglected; the hope of the poor will not be crushed forever. PSALM 9:18

When we have truly taken the First Step and admitted our powerlessness, the relief we feel is so overwhelming, we want to rush out and tell those we know that they should do what we have done. The same thing happens after the Second and Third Steps. The excitement we feel with each step of our spiritual journey often energizes us to convince all those we know, especially those who seem to be having any sort of problem, that we have the solution.

The writers of the Twelve Steps wisely put the task of carrying the message last. Until we are firmly grounded in the other Eleven Steps, we are not ready to tell anyone anything. We are too apt to analyze, judge, and attempt to control. We are too apt to lapse into self-righteousness if we are successful or into self-doubt if we fail. The temptation to play god can be overwhelming.

But finally we will be ready, and then we can be used to help the needy of the world.

May God make us ready to take the Twelfth Step.

July 31

You have changed my sadness into a joyful dance; you have taken away my sorrow and surrounded me with joy. PSALM 30:11

Our relationship to a true lover takes time to grow. In the early stages, we share the safe information. But as we become more and more secure in the other's love, we begin sharing the deep, intimate details, the little secrets that let the other know how to love us better, how to respond to us in ways that fulfill both lover and beloved. Our hearts fill with the joy of one deeply loved when our lover gives us gifts that indicate his or her intimate knowledge of us.

Our relationship to our Source develops in the same way. We begin by sharing our obvious problems, letting God help us with the things we cannot do for ourselves. But, we hold onto our secrets. Then, little by little, we grow in our willingness to share our deepest yearnings with God. And soon our hearts are filled with joy by the intimate gifts God gives us.

May our relationship to the Source of our being become deeper and more intimate.

august

August 1

My strength is gone, gone like water spilled on the ground. All my bones are out of joint; my heart is like melted wax. PSALM 22:14

This poetic image of what it feels like to be suffering from spiritual dis-ease reflects a common condition. We have all had times when we have felt exhausted, out of joint, heartsick. In addition to these symptoms, there are many other symptoms of spiritual dis-ease. Perhaps we feel as if there is a river of tears dammed up behind our eyes, ready to overflow at the least provocation. Or maybe we strike out in anger over little things that should not have bothered us. Sometimes our bodies react with unexplained headaches or digestive problems.

Whenever we recognize symptoms that could be signs of spiritual dis-ease, we need to ask ourselves, "In what areas am I trying to control something that is not mine to control?" "Where am I trying to exert power rather than letting God be God?"

Admitting our powerlessness in those areas and redirecting our energies can relieve the symptoms and restore spiritual health.

May God help us recognize symptoms signaling that all is not well with our spirits.

August 2

Don't put me, your servant, on trial; no one is innocent in your sight. PSALM 143:2

Innocent or guilty, to be on trial is a fearsome experience. Whether that trial takes place in a courtroom or in a relationship, a case is brought against us. We stand accused, blamed. The experience usually brings out the worst in us. Often we become defensive, rationalizing our behavior and pointing to others who are clearly worse than we are. Or we try to turn the tables, finding fault with our accuser. We may even turn on ourselves, accepting all the blame and falling into self-deprecation and despair.

Failure exists on both sides in any relationship. The closer and more intimate the relationship, the more possibility there is for failure. "No one is innocent," not we ourselves and not the others in our lives. One of the greatest gifts we can give is to stop putting ourselves or each other on trial, stop blaming, and learn to live with a gracious acceptance of our own imperfections and those of others.

May our Creator remove from us the tendency to blame and fill us with acceptance of ourselves and others.

August 3

They couldn't stand the sight of food and were close to death. Then in their trouble they called to the Lord, and God saved them from their distress. PSALM 107:18–19

For those who have struggled with the disease of anorexia, this verse rings literally true. Food, that substance we most need to maintain life, becomes abhorrent, giving free reign to our self-destructive impulse.

"Food" can also be a symbol of any basic need – the need for love, for security, for meaning, for physical and emotional intimacy. If we reach a point where we refuse to try to satisfy any one of those needs, we begin to move "close to death." We become overwhelmed by a sense of isolation, of loneliness, of longing. And yet we cut ourselves off from anything that could give us the nourishment we need.

At these points in our lives, that part of ourselves that seeks to destroy us is winning the inner struggle. We are powerless to do anything except call to God for help. And God has promised to save us so that we can grow toward wholeness.

May God empower us to work for our own well-being.

August 4

"You relied on the Lord," they say. "Why haven't you been saved? If the Lord likes you, why haven't you been helped?" PSALM 22:8

When the child was six years old, her father became ill. She prayed with all the fervor of a child who believed that God loved her and answered prayer. But her father died. It was as if scales fell from her eyes. All around her she saw pain and suffering. She asked "Why?" and was told it was God's will. She asked again and was told she needed more faith. She responded with anger and bitterness.

But somewhere within her, that voice of love kept calling her name. Years later, when her life had reached its lowest ebb, she called out in desperation, "You failed me before. Can you help me now?"

The voice responded, "Look around you again. What do you see?" Again she felt as if scales were falling from her eyes. She could see how God had touched her life in many ways through friends and family. And she came to believe that God could help her.

May we feel the assurance of God's involvement in our lives.

August 5

Don't put your trust in human leaders; no human being can save you. PSALM 146:3

We live in an age of cynicism about political leaders, doctors, teachers, clergy, and even loved ones and friends. Our experience has taught us not to trust them. Our minds tell us that they are fallible human beings, as apt to make mistakes as we are.

And yet there is a part of us that yearns for a human "savior," that perfect person who will know exactly what we need when we need it and be able to give it to us. We spend much of our lives searching for that person, placing our expectations on one friend after another, one professional after another, one family member after another. When they fail us, as they always do, we blame them and feel bitterly disappointed. We cry about broken trust and dashed dreams.

But the problem was not with the other. It was with our misplaced expectation, our misdirected yearning. No other person can save us. We are all struggling together, all in need of a God who saves.

May God free us from the yearning for a human "savior."

August 6

I remember the days gone by; I think about all that you have done, I bring to mind all your deeds. PSALM 143:5

The Israelite nation sometimes had to survive for hundreds of years without any direct, unmistakable action by God. It was easy to become discouraged, to wonder if God had left them, or if there even was a God. During those times they had to rely on their memories and the stories they had heard. "Remember when God delivered us from slavery." "Remember when God saved us from the Philistines."

The woman sat curled in a chair in a stark room of a drug treatment center. She had just poured out her life story, a story of being abused and abusing others, of being used and using others, of being hurt and hurting others. There seemed to be no indication of God in her life anywhere. Then someone asked, "Has anything good happened to you?" Thoughtfully, she replied, "I'm alive. I could have been dead so many times. And I'm here. I still can't believe I'm here." Someday she may see God's involvement in that reality, and the memory will help her endure the difficult struggles still ahead.

May God help us see God's work in our lives.

August 7

The Lord is with me, I will not be afraid; what can anyone do to me? PSALM 118:6

To know that our God is with us, that we do not need to be afraid, ought to be enough. But, like Eve in the garden, we want to know more. We want to know exactly what God is doing in our lives and why. We especially want to know where it all will lead. What is going to happen? Will it be difficult? Will it hurt? Will we lose any of the things that are so important to us? We pick apart each event of our lives, analyzing what God is doing, perhaps even judging our Creator's effectiveness.

When we make a decision to turn our lives over to the care of God, all we are guaranteed is that our Protector and Deliverer will be with us and that, therefore, we do not need to be afraid. Such knowledge allows us to live freely and fearlessly in the moment, observing and experiencing God's involvement in our lives without needing to know the end result. Taking the Third Step allows us truly to live one day at a time.

May our awareness of God's presence in our lives free us to live each day to its fullest.

August 8

I call to the Lord for help, I plead. I bring God all my complaints; I tell God all my troubles. PSALM 142:1-2

All parents know how good it feels when their children confide in them about their troubles. They are also complimented and affirmed when their children ask for help or advice. But listening to complaints by children, or anyone for that matter, is quite another thing. Complaints are like the sound of a dripping faucet. Our first impulse is to do whatever we can to shut it off.

The psalmist tells us about a relationship with a God who not only listens to our troubles and calls for help, but also listens to complaints. Nothing is too trivial for God. God may not enjoy listening to complaining any more than a parent does, but still God listens, knowing how important it is for us to be heard and taken seriously.

The model is an important one to remember the next time family members, friends, or coworkers begin to complain. Listening to them and taking them seriously may be all they need to get beyond their complaints and on to more productive thinking.

May the Comforter of all give us listening ears.

August 9

In the shadow of your wings I find protection until the raging storms are over. PSALM 57:1B

The eaglet huddled in its eyrie high on a cliff in the Rocky Mountains as the storm's intensity increased. The small bird need not have feared. Its mother instinctively knew the danger and was on her way back to the nest with a fish in her claw. As the storm raged all around, whipping snow and sleet onto the mother, the eaglet, warm and safe under her wings, ate its dinner and slept.

It is God's desire and pleasure to shelter us from the storms of our lives, protecting our lives as a mother bird spreads her wings and protects her young. The storms still rage, the winds still blow, the snow and sleet still sting, but we are safe if we remain under God's powerful wings.

But God cannot force us into the nest. And sometimes our own pride, lack of trust, or stubborn willfulness, keep us out on the cliff, alone, trying to survive the storm. All we need do is return to the nest.

May we find protection in the shadow of God's wings.

August 10

I kept quiet, not saying a word, not even about anything good! But my suffering only grew worse, and I was overcome with anxiety. PSALM 39:2

Many of us have suffered from the kind of anxiety the psalmist is talking about, the kind of anxiety that comes from holding it all in. For a variety of reasons, there are times in our lives when we think we cannot tell anyone what we are feeling. These feelings, if left inside, work their way out in many ways, including anxiety, irrational anger, or physical problems.

One of the side benefits of doing a Fourth Step is that we take what is inside of us and bring it to the outside, writing down both what is good and what is bad. The process of writing helps us know what we are thinking and feeling. It also helps us objectify those thoughts and feelings, see them as something separate from ourselves that we can, at this point, deal with more rationally. The paper on which we write becomes a mirror in which we take a careful, nonjudgmental look at ourselves and discover an interesting, loveable person.

May God embrace us as we bring what is inside out.

August 11

May his creditors take away all his property. . . . May no one ever be kind to him or care for the orphans he leaves behind. PSALM 109:11-12

It is disturbing to read the many psalms that are filled with this kind of vindictiveness. We have been taught to believe that it is bad to want to get even with those who hurt us. We assume that even thinking such thoughts is a mark of spiritual inadequacy, and so we hide them even from ourselves.

The problem is that hidden thoughts or feelings do not remain hidden. They simply go underground long enough to create a disguise for themselves and then they reappear, provoking actions that are irresponsible and irrational.

The wonder of these psalms is that they give us permission to feel and to express the anger we feel toward someone who has behaved in hurtful ways toward us or toward those we love. They do not, however, give us permission to act on that anger by returning evil for evil. Before we can let go of vindictive feelings, we need to honestly claim them, and then recognize that it is not helpful for us to hold onto them.

May God help us let go of vindictive feelings.

August 12

God sets the time for love and the time for hate, the time for war and the time for peace. ECCLESIASTES 3:8

This is the final verse in the well-known series of verses in Ecclesiastes that describes the polarities of life and God's control of these polarities. The verses following tell how humans can neither understand these polarities nor predict them. All we can do is experience them, searching for and treasuring the unique blessings that each brings.

These verses stand as a monument to all that is out of our control, to all over which we are powerless. They remind us of our vulnerability. They tell us that there is no such thing as security. We do not know what tomorrow will bring. Neither do we know if we will ever see the results of what we do today.

To live for the future (in fear or hope), to struggle to make ourselves "secure," to consider today as preparation for tomorrow is to miss the point of biblical wisdom. All we have is today, now. Our task is to treasure the day, cherishing ourselves in it.

May our Deliverer free us to live for today.

August 13

This is how unfaithful spouses act: they commit adultery, take a bath, and say, "But I haven't done anything wrong!" PROVERBS 30:20

There is a big difference between being forgiven for our wrongdoing and going through some sort of rationalization process that lifts our guilt by convincing us that we really did not do anything wrong. One process frees us, the other constricts us. One process draws us close to God and others, the other deepens the gulf that keeps us separate.

We fool ourselves if we think we will feel better about ourselves by finding ways to avoid saying, "I was wrong," "I was unfaithful," "I deeply hurt another human being." Our rationalizations are like bandages over a burn. They prevent the healing. Eventually the burn will become infected and begin poisoning our self-esteem and our relationships at levels we cannot control.

Healing can begin only when we label wrongdoing for what it is, ask for forgiveness, and set about changing our ways.

May God help us strip off the bandage of rationalization.

August 14

I have sinned against you—only against you—and done what you consider evil. So you are right in judging me; you are justified in condemning me. PSALM 51:4

Marie had been pouring out her guilt for what seemed like hours. She had talked about all of the relationships in her life, confessing the ways in which she had hurt others, either through her actions or through her attitudes. Then she heard the soft voice of the woman hearing her Fifth Step say, "Now, think about your spiritual life, about God. How have you hurt yourself?"

Marie's first thought was of all the ways that God had hurt her, had let her down, had not protected her from all the terrible things that had happened to her. But as she talked, she realized that the bad things she had experienced were mostly a result of her own bad choices. And she could not blame God for them. Then she realized that blaming God was another bad choice, another way in which she was hurting herself. All she could see was her failure. But her Creator saw something different—a wonderful woman, open and ready for a new life.

May we see ourselves as our Creator sees us.

August 15

Then in their trouble they called to the Lord, and God saved them from their distress, bringing them out of their gloom and darkness and breaking their chains in pieces. PSALM 107:13-14

These verses combine three powerful images of what it is like to live without the power of God in our lives or in specific areas of our lives. The first is the image of gloom. We all know what a gloomy day is like or how it is to feel gloomy. It is as if all colors were grey, all sounds monotone, all tastes like gruel. Our emotions are low and flat.

Life without the power of God is also like living in darkness. We feel frightened and timid, fearing we will trip over rocks in our path or fall into pits we cannot see.

The final image is of living bound by chains, held down, diminished, constricted. Such living is the opposite of freedom, the antithesis of love.

The good thing about gloom, darkness and chains is that they make us uncomfortable enough to really want things different. And God can save us from our distress.

May God bring light and freedom to all parts of our lives.

August 16

You do not want sacrifices . . . to take away sins. Instead, you have given me ears to hear you, and so I answered, "Here I am. . . ." PSALM 40:6B–7A

In the culture in which the psalmist was writing, people brought an animal or offering of some sort as a sacrifice in order to be forgiven for their sins. It was often seen as a payment or punishment for the sin. But, God wanted them to sacrifice animals as a sign that they were sacrificing the sin, that they were giving up the wrong behavior.

The Sixth Step involves preparing ourselves for this sacrifice, and that is not always easy. Our negative behaviors always have some positive benefits. Infidelity brings us the thrill of a new love, the passion of illicit sex. Self-righteousness gives us a sense of superiority. Envy allows us to avoid dealing with our real needs by letting us assume that if we just had what others have, we would be fine. Every defect in our character has a short-term reward that we need to be willing to sacrifice along with the defect. Being ready takes work on our part and help from God.

May God make us ready to sacrifice our wrong behaviors.

August 17

[Good people] are not afraid of receiving bad news; their faith is strong, and they trust in the Lord. PSALM 112:7

When the phone rings late at night, our hearts skip a beat. Who has died? Who is in trouble? How will our lives be changed? We all have had such calls and know how devastating they can be, and so we live in fear of receiving bad news. Sometimes that fear can be disabling, disturbing our nights, hampering our days.

Bad news will come when it will come. Our challenge is to learn to live without fear of the future. The psalmist describes people who are not afraid of receiving bad news and then answers the question, "How can they live that way?" with the words, "Their faith is strong, and they trust in the Lord."

As we continue on our faith journey, it is good to spend some time reflecting on where we have been, noting how God has guided us, helped us, and empowered us. Learning to recognize God's hand in our pasts will enable us more and more to trust God with our futures. And, as trust increases, fear decreases.

May our faith and trust grow stronger this day.

August 18

Whenever I am filled with cares, your comfort sooths my soul. PSALM 94:19

We have all been given a birthright by God. It is the gift of love, of personal worth, of ultimate care and protection, of comfort. But most of us, like Esau (Genesis 25:27-34), have forfeited our birthright for a quick bowl of food to fill us at a moment of great hunger.

The problem is not that we cannot reclaim what is ours by right (God has never taken back the gift). The problem is that the habit of finding a "quick fix"—someone or something to make us feel better immediately—forms quickly, and we forget that there is another way, that we have a birthright.

When the psalmist was filled with cares, he might have taken a pill, had a drink, eaten obsessively, or gone on a shopping spree, but instead he claimed his birthright. He may have used the scriptures, prayer, meditation, or all three. Whatever he did, he found comfort through directly claiming what was his by right—the love of God. And so can we.

May we reclaim the birthright God has given us.

August 19

Be patient and wait for the Lord to act. PSALM 37:7A

The woman was always critical of others. She could not seem to stop herself. At meetings she would think and often say cruel things that demonstrated her lack of acceptance of others. At home, no matter what others in her family did, she would think and usually say something negative.

Hating this trait in herself, she began asking God to remove it. She waited impatiently, but there seemed to be no improvement. She could not understand what she was doing wrong, why God did not help her. She poured out her frustration to a friend, who said lovingly, "Why do you think you need to be so critical?" She looked beneath the surface and realized that her critical attitude masked her own feelings of worthlessness. How could she love and accept others if she could not love and accept herself?

She started over, praying that the Source of her life would lift her self-esteem and help her love herself. That was the defect that needed to be removed before the other defect could be dealt with.

May the Source of our being give us insight into ourselves as we seek to have our shortcomings removed.

August 20

Keep company with the wise and you will become wise. If you make friends with stupid people, you will be ruined. PROVERBS 13:20

The message in this verse seems so simple on the surface. Of course, if possible, we would want to keep company with wise people. And, of course, we would not want to make friends with those who are stupid. The problem is, how do we know the difference?

We have all been in situations where we have been very impressed with and influenced by another who seemed wise—a parent, friend, teacher, counselor, doctor—only to discover later that the advice we took or the ideas we accepted worked against us.

Perhaps the beginning of wisdom is the realization that no other person really knows us or knows what is best for us. Only God does. When in the company of the truly wise, we discover that very little advice is given or taken. There is a humble recognition that there are no easy answers. In fact, there are no answers. We walk through life with one hand holding our questions and the other held by God.

May God help us choose wise friends.

August 21

My eyes are tired from watching for what you promised, while I ask, "When will you help me?" PSALM 119:82

Recognizing the limitations of human advice and human wisdom and turning to God for help can be a frustrating experience. We find ourselves echoing the words of the psalmist, "When will you help me? I am tired of waiting." We cry to God, "I want help now. I want change now. You've promised to make my life better, to make me better, and nothing seems to be any different. In fact, sometimes things are worse."

Recovering from addiction of any kind is a little like having your tonsils out. Even though you suffer from sore throats or colds, you could go on living indefinitely with bad tonsils. But once you decide you do not want to live that way anymore, you agree to surgery—a time when your pain and suffering increase, but the healing, however slow, follows. Only then can life get better.

We do not understand God's timing or the ways in which God performs "surgery." We can only trust that someday we will look back and realize that, yes, our lives are better.

May God give us patience and hope.

August 22

If you want people to like you, forgive them when they wrong you. Remembering wrongs can break up a friendship. PROVERBS 17:9

As we work on the Eighth Step, making a list of the people we have wronged, it is easy to overlook those relationships where others have clearly wronged us. We rationalize away our resentment and lack of forgiveness by saying, "He hurt me and hasn't admitted it," or "When she admits her part, I'll admit mine."

It is important to remember that we are not responsible for another's spiritual journey. Our focus is ourselves. If we have not forgiven someone, if we have held onto a resentment no matter how justified it may seem, then we have wronged both ourselves and the other, and it is our responsibility to make amends.

When we combine the concept of forgiveness with the slogan "One day at a time," we can learn to let go of all that happened in the past and live in the present, free from the strain that comes from holding onto resentment.

May God empower us to forgive persons who have wronged us.

August 23

Getting involved in an argument that is none of your business is like going down the street and grabbing a dog by the ears. PROVERBS 26:17

The writer observes that we will likely get hurt if we become involved in an argument that is none of our business. And yet we do it all the time. At work we try to analyze and fix the squabbles of our co-workers. At home we jump into the middle of disagreements between family members, trying to control the outcome. We set ourselves up as arbitrators of arguments between friends. It seems clear that they need our help. They, after all, have lost all perspective and common sense.

But what happens when we get involved? First of all, it rarely helps settle the argument. We just add another complicating factor. We toss more volatile feelings into the already burning pot.

Not only do we usually make the argument worse, but we put ourselves in a position where we will likely be attacked, rejected, or ignored. And then we feel sorry for ourselves. We were, after all, just trying to help.

May our Creator give us restraint and good judgment.

August 24

A person's words can be a source of wisdom, deep as the ocean, fresh as a flowing stream. PROVERBS 18:4

The process of making amends (the Ninth Step) usually has four parts: facing the person and admitting the wrong (unless to do so would injure them or others), apologizing, making restitution if possible, and changing our behavior so that we are no longer acting in those hurtful ways. The interaction is often very powerful, our words being "fresh as a flowing stream," restoring life to our souls and love to our relationships.

Forgiveness is a prerequisite for loving. Before we attempt to make amends, it is important that we have forgiven ourselves for our mistakes and also the other person for any wrong that person may have done to us. If our Ninth-Step amends are built on forgiveness of ourselves, forgiveness of the other, and a deep, honest desire to be forgiven *by* the other, then those amends can open the door for the flow of life-giving love. This love washes away all bitterness, resentment, anger, and hate.

May the Source of life make our amends a life-giving stream.

August 25

Why am I so sad? Why am I so troubled? I will put my hope in God, and once again I will praise my savior and my God. PSALM 42:5

For the psalmist, the feelings of being sad or being troubled signaled a spiritual problem—loss of hope. The Tenth Step—a daily inventory—is our way of taking our spiritual temperature and, if it is not normal (serenity has now become the norm), trying to diagnose what the problem is. The symptoms to watch for include anger, self-pity, worry, resentment, envy, jealousy, depression, fear, dishonesty, arrogance, greed, loss of self-control, impatience, intolerance, the desire to get even.

These symptoms indicate spiritual dis-ease. They are like a fever, telling us that all is not well within. They must always be taken seriously and never accepted as normal or "human" or they will spread, infecting all parts of our emotional and spiritual being. These symptoms might indicate that we have taken back our wills. Or, perhaps they are a sign that we have some talent, some unused gift, that is crying to be expressed. We have not let ourselves grow to our potential.

May our Healer alert us to signs of spiritual dis-ease.

August 26

Pride goes before ruin, arrogance, before failure.
PROVERBS 16:18

When she was a child, she was always told it was important to be best at everything she did. But whenever she accomplished anything, her mother would remind her, "Pride goes before ruin. . . ." The message was clear. It was important to do well, but it was more important to never feel good about her accomplishments and never, ever brag to anyone else.

In fact, the pride that leads to ruin has nothing to do with feeling good about ourselves or enjoying what we do well. It is the opposite. Destructive pride is rooted in our obsession with what others think of us. We do all things with the goal that we will be regarded as intelligent, competent, powerful, affluent, clever, . . . We keep our focus on others, trying to control or manipulate their attitudes toward us. We mask our defects and become angry and resentful when others criticize us or stand in our way. In other words, destructive pride cuts off the flow of love to ourselves, to others, and to God.

May God fill us with good feelings about ourselves.

August 27

I am unimportant and despised, but I do not neglect your teachings. PSALM 119:141

Taken out of context, this verse has a very self-pitying sound—"I know that I am nothing, but I try." It is the sort of thing we say when we need affirmation, when we want our friends or family members to pat us on the back and tell us how wonderful we are.

But taken within the context of the psalm, it is clearly not self-pity. The writer loves the teachings of God even though they have brought him neither status nor respect. He has reached a point in his spiritual journey where listening to God and walking in God's ways are enough to bring him contentment. He does not need external proof or reward.

Such a state of being seems impossible for those of us still struggling with nagging doubt, the need for proof, and the desire to see God at work. But as we diligently learn spiritual principles and practice spiritual disciplines, and as we struggle to know more and more about God, we will discover that this is enough.

May we be filled with love for God's teachings.

August 28

More than once I have heard God say that power belongs to God and that the Lord's love is constant.
PSALM 62:11

As we daily take the Eleventh Step, we are reminded over and over again that we do not know what is best for us. There is no way that we can project into the future and know that a particular happening, a particular relationship, a particular job, will be best for us. Neither do we know that relief or escape from the troubles with which we are currently living will be best for us. We do not know.

But God, whose love is constant, knows and wants to guide us. Our task is to get our self-will out of the way so that we can listen. So we pray for knowledge of God's will for us.

We also pray for power to carry out that will. The psalmist says that all power belongs to God. As is true of any good parent, God wants to give us everything we need to live whole lives. And so we pray for power, trusting that we will be given all we need to carry out God's will for us today.

May God help us strip away self-will, leaving us open to receive guidance and power.

August 29

But God takes pleasure in those who honor him, in those who trust in God's constant love. PSALM 147:11

It is odd, almost absurd, to think that God, who created all things, who controls the universe, who is beyond all human understanding and questioning, could be interested in me, one speck in the creation. But to go even further and state that this God, who is so far beyond anything that I can imagine, takes pleasure when I demonstrate honor and trust seems ridiculous. And yet that is what the psalmist tells us.

One way to understand this is to use the image or metaphor of God as a parent. No matter how many children a good parent has, each child is loved and nurtured individually. And the parent takes great pleasure when each child reaches the stage where she or he responds to the parent with trust and honor. So it is with God—not only a supreme being or a higher power, but a heavenly mother or father who responds with joy when we hold out our arms in trust.

May we sense God's pleasure as we grow in love and trust.

August 30

Make my enemies know that you are the one who saves me. PSALM 109:27

We do not know what the psalmist has gone through to reach this point, but clearly he has been through a very difficult time and has been saved, been freed, been brought to the other side. He is at the point where we are when we begin trying to work the Twelfth Step. But he did not fall into the trap that is so easy for us to fall into — taking credit for our own recovery, especially among people who do not understand the process of recovery.

As we set about practicing the principles of spiritual recovery that we have learned and experienced "in all our affairs," we encounter all kinds of situations and people who can, potentially, bring out the worst in us. At these times, even a touch of pride, a whisper of "I did it myself, aren't I great?" can be like a trap, plunging us back into our addictions.

With the psalmist, we need to remember that we could have done nothing without God. It is God who saves us.

May our Protector keep us from the trap of pride.

August 31

They will speak of your glory and majesty, and I will meditate on your wonderful deeds. PSALM 145:5

The woman went from friend to friend, from group to group, trying to find someone who would listen to her tell about all that God had done for her. She wanted to describe how bad her life had been and how she had finally turned her life over to God. She was filled to overflowing with love and gratitude for a God who had worked such a miracle in her life.

But no one seemed to want to listen. Either their eyes would turn bitter and envious or they would break in, telling about all their problems as a way of refuting her contention that God was at work. Or they would interrupt, topping her story with one of their own. All she wanted was for someone to listen and rejoice with her, but even those who had had similar experiences seemed unable to do so.

The psalmist tells of speakers and listeners, of those who tell of what God has done and those who accept these stories without envy, letting them nurture their own faith. We give an incredible gift to another when we listen.

May our listening nurture both ourselves and others.

september

September 1

But even darkness is not dark for you, and the night is as bright as the day. Darkness and light are the same to you. PSALM 139:12

Darkness and light, night and day. For those of us who have felt darkness descend into our souls, these words are opposites. We fear inner darkness, we dread the nighttime of our spirits, and we cling to the last rays of twilight when we sense that night is coming again. These are the times when we feel untouched by love, either from God or from others, and we cannot love ourselves. Sometimes the darkness becomes so thick, so intense, that our spiritual eyes begin to adjust. We begin to assume that darkness is the only reality, that there is no light, no love, no hope. And we settle back into the emptiness.

But the psalmist tells us that "darkness and light are the same" to God. Our Creator knows that the nighttimes of our souls are a necessary prelude to the dawn. There is hope in the darkness. God is there, at work, preparing us for a new day.

May our Helper bring us through our darkness and into light.

September 2

I lie awake; I am like a lonely bird on a housetop.
PSALM 102:7

Perched alone on a housetop, a bird can neither mate nor nest nor feed. But the bird can see longer distances and with greater clarity than when it is busy with the instinctive routines of its life.

Often when we lie awake at night, unable to sleep, our minds spin with worry, plans, or fears. We dredge up all the pain from the past or play out in our minds all the worst things that could happen in the future. And if we cannot find anything else to fret about, we worry because we are not sleeping.

But no life situation is beyond redemption—even sleeplessness. If we can silence our mind chatter long enough, we can use that time to focus on God in prayer, to meditate on our Creator's will, to let the Source of life expand our vision so that we can see farther and with greater clarity. It is sometimes hard for God to catch our attention during the busyness of the day, but in the quiet of the night, when sleep will not visit us, God can and will come.

May we be touched by God during the quiet of the night.

September 3

My throat is as dry as dust, and my tongue sticks to the roof of my mouth. PSALM 22:15A

The image painted by the psalmist can be taken literally as a description of a physical problem, or it can be taken metaphorically, describing an inability to connect with others through meaningful speech. We have all had times when we yearned for companionship and intimacy, but somehow what we said worked against us rather than for us.

During these times we often distance ourselves from those closest to us, hurt those we love, blame or judge persons who are trying to help us. Everything we say or do makes us feel worse — guilty and alone. Our problem has its roots in our spirit, and its symptoms affect all of our interpersonal relationships.

Recognizing any of these symptoms in our lives reminds us to go back to the First Step. We need to take a good, hard look at ourselves and admit that at least some parts of our lives are out of control and need to be turned over to God.

May our Protector alert us to danger signals in our spiritual journeys.

September 4

I am worn out from calling for help, and my throat is aching. I have strained my eyes, looking for your help. PSALM 69:3

It was 20° below zero. Strong, northerly winds whipped thick snow across the highway. The small car she was driving was no match for the weather. On a particularly barren stretch, she was blown into the ditch, where drifts began forming around her car. She left on her lights and blinkers hoping a passing motorist would see her, but her battery went dead. Then, frantic, she tried getting out of the car to go for help, but she succeeded only in filling the car with freezing air and snow. Helpless and without hope, she wrapped herself in a blanket and prepared to sleep into death.

The next thing she knew, she was being lifted from her car by a concerned farmer. "I saw you going down, but I had to get my tractor going and get here." She was not alone. Help had been on the way from the beginning. Her frantic efforts to help herself had only made things worse.

May we grow in our assurance that we are being cared for by God.

September 5

You have given us our heart's desire, you have answered our requests. PSALM 21:2

It is easy for us to think that the good things that happen to us (material possessions, good relationships, health, education, security) are a just reward for all that we have done. We even slide into thinking that they are our right, and we feel sorry for ourselves, blaming God, ourselves, or others when we do not have them.

The process of coming to believe that a power greater than ourselves can help us (the Second Step) often begins with a conscious effort to see these good things as gifts from our Creator, gifts given because we are loved. "Thank you, God, that I am alive and that some or all of my body is in good health. Thank you for a place to sleep, enough food to sustain me, people who care about me, opportunity." Beginning each day by making a list of all we have to be thankful for is a good way to turn our thinking away from self-pity or blame and toward gratitude – acknowledgment of a God who is actively working for good in our lives.

May God give us a spirit of gratitude.

September 6

When I am ready to give up, God knows what I should do. PSALM 142:3A

Of course, God knows what we should do all along, but it is often only when we are ready to give up, when we have exhausted all of our own ideas, when all of our own plans have met with failure and we do not know where to turn, that we turn to our Maker. And even when we turn to God, we sometimes do so, not looking for help, but in anger and blame for our troubles and for not making things work out the way we wanted.

But God, like a patient and loving parent, waits. When our frenetic activity is over, when our anger has dissipated, when we realize that we cannot control or fix or even plan, when we finally trust God enough to put our lives in God's hands, then things can start to change for the better. Our Creator is ready to give us a vision of what we can do, nudge us in the right direction, and empower us to move forward. God's creative efforts in us can continue, transforming us into strong, courageous, powerful people.

May God create new strength in us.

September 7

The Lord watches over those who have reverence, those who trust in God's constant love. PSALM 33:18

God can be like our counselor – that person we go to with our problems, pouring out all our pain and looking for help in understanding and decision making. In fact, it is easy to use God in this way and think we are taking the Third Step. We practice the slogan, "Let go and let God," by turning over to God those problem areas of our lives that we finally realize we cannot fix ourselves.

But the Third Step is much, much more. It may begin with a relinquishing of one part of our lives or another, but it is not complete until we have turned all of ourselves over to the care of God – even those parts that are not problems. This lifelong process involves our value systems, all our relationships, our daily tasks, our hopes and dreams, the way we talk, the way we make and use our money, the way we work, the activities we become involved in. When we truly trust in God's constant love, there is no part of our lives that we want to keep separate from that love. And so we turn our whole life over to God.

May we feel our God watching over us with constant love.

September 8

You answered me when I called to you; with your strength you strengthened me. PSALM 138:3

People often have great resistance to turning their lives over to their Highest Power, fearing that they will then become less than human in some way. Either they will be like puppets dancing on the end of strings held by God, with no personality of their own, or they will become lazy, irresponsible do-nothings, sitting around waiting for God to do for them what they ought to be doing for themselves.

But, in fact, quite the opposite is true. When we relinquish hold on our lives, God can set about making us more truly ourselves, more deeply human. Our Creator wants to empower us to use our gifts to their fullest potential, to walk with courage, and to be strong. It is God's desire that we not fear failure or criticism or ridicule, that we not crave success or attention or affirmation, that we not be controlled by an insatiable need for food or chemicals or work. It is our Deliverer's plan that we walk free – loving, loved, and loveable – quite the opposite of being a puppet.

May our lives be empowered by our Creator.

September 9

It is better to trust in the Lord than to depend on human leaders. PSALM 118:9

We live in a culture that sets independence as an attainable goal in the same way that it markets security as something we can have. And yet both these concepts are illusions. Trying to attain them inevitably leads to disillusionment.

We are, in fact, a part of an interdependent network, all parts of which must be working in order for us to live reasonably safe, secure lives. We are dependent on doctors, political leaders, law enforcement people, and technicians of every sort. Any error or deliberate wrongdoing by one of a million unknown people, and our lives could be destroyed or dramatically altered at any time.

How can one live confidently and fearlessly when there is so much to fear? Common sense helps—taking logical precautions and then recognizing that we cannot control everything. It also helps to look back and realize that we have survived difficult times. But the most important ingredient for confident living is knowing that we are in the strong and loving hands of God.

May our Deliverer free us from feelings of fear and insecurity.

September 10

I am drowning in the flood of my sins; they are a burden too heavy to bear. PSALM 38:4

For all of us who feel as if we are "drowning in the flood" of our sins, working on the Fourth Step is like climbing onto a life raft. In that raft, we can separate ourselves from the flood, take a deep breath, and look at our situations and ourselves objectively.

Sometimes it takes weeks or even months in our raft before we have a good idea of the breadth and depth of the flood. But the amazing thing about a Fourth Step is that the more honest we are about ourselves and our situations and the more willing we are to take responsibility for our behavior, the more apt the flood is to recede even as we watch. Before long it becomes clear where the high ground is, where the safe paths are, where we can walk without risk. It also becomes clear where our sinkholes are, our whirlpools, our drop-offs. Knowing ourselves is a most important part of our spiritual journey.

May our Helper rescue us from the flood of our own behavior and lift us to dry ground.

September 11

If you wait until the wind and the weather are just right, you will never plant anything and never harvest anything. ECCLESIASTES 11:4

Procrastination is a dangerous character trait in many of us. We excuse ourselves for not doing a wide variety of important things by saying that the time is not right or tomorrow would be better. This bad habit infects our daily tasks, our relationships, and our spiritual journeys.

In Twelve-Step groups, there are any number of people who have never actually done a Fourth Step even though they have read about it and talked about it for years. If we do not plant, neither can we harvest. Without that time of painful introspection, we cannot go on to the relief of the Fifth Step or the life-changing power of the rest of the Steps.

While, on the one hand, timing is important (there is a good time and a less good time for everything), on the other hand, if we are looking for excuses for not doing something, we can always find them.

May God free us of the tendency to procrastinate in all areas of our lives.

September 12

God changed the sea into dry land; our ancestors crossed the river on foot. Therefore we rejoice because of what God did. PSALM 66:6

The Israelites rejoiced because they had been given freedom from the bondage of slavery and saved from the Egyptians who were pursuing them. But it was not long before they were complaining. While slavery was not much fun, it was secure and predictable. Freedom was neither.

Each time we give up the bondage of one of our addictions, we move into a stage of great insecurity where the evil that we once had begins to look preferable to the fearful unknown. The giving up of an addiction might mean drastic altering of our friendships. The people who liked us before might not like us now. We might need to look for other employment or find new things to do with our long evening hours. Destructive as our addictions were, still they were familiar. We felt at home with them. Any change, especially freedom, plunges us into the unknown.

But we will learn, as the Israelites did, that God is ready and waiting to give us manna for the day.

May God lead us to freedom, nourishing us along the way.

September 13

May those who rejoice at my misfortune be frustrated and utterly disgraced. PSALM 35:26B

The psalmist reflects on a common human trait—resentment toward those who in any way claim superiority over us, and a perverse desire to see those people disgraced. Being in a position where we feel as if others are looking down on us often brings out the worst in us—envy, self-pity, resentment, self-justification, even revenge. We want those people punished for their arrogance and brought low so that we can look down on them.

When we find ourselves thinking this way, we need to quickly catch ourselves. We are wounding our own spirits by letting the attitude of another affect us. The spiritual issue is one of trust—we do not trust that our own life experiences are in God's hands. Neither do we trust that God is working in the lives of those people we resent, loving them and trying to create in them a more loving, accepting spirit. Naming and admitting our resentments can free us from their grip and rekindle love toward self and others.

May God heal the wounds to our spirits caused by resentment.

September 14

God does not punish us as we deserve or repay us for our sins and wrongs. PSALM 103:10

"Is God punishing me?" the woman asked, tears of anger and pain welling up in her eyes. "Do you deserve to be punished?" her friend and spiritual mentor asked gently. The woman broke, guilt and anguish pouring out of her eyes and through her words as she began recounting all of the things in her life that she had done wrong and all of the pain that had resulted.

Her friend waited for the sobbing to subside and then began talking. "What God has told us not to do, those things we call sins, are sins because they build walls within us and around us. They hurt us and hurt others and sever the flow of love. Our Creator does not want us to have to live that way. We always pay a price for doing things that are wrong, but it is not God who is punishing us. God's greatest desire is that we live free of guilt, free from walls that shut us in and others out, free to love and be loved." The woman lifted her eyes as her friend went on, "God has forgiven you. And God can help you forgive yourself."

May God lift from us the weight of guilt.

September 15

Be merciful to me, O God, because of your constant love. Because of your great mercy wipe away my sins!
PSALM 51:1

A part of being ready to have God remove our defects of character is having such a deep trust relationship with our Creator that we are not afraid of the kind of changes that will take place in us. We pray to God to be merciful to us – not to give us what we deserve, but what we need; not to alter us in ways that we will not like, but to make us more free than we have ever been.

Sometimes we have an image of the "perfect person" and assume that is the way God wants us to be. That person is often too good, too righteous, too perfect for anyone to feel comfortable with. We do not want to be like that, so we fear losing our humanity by having our defects removed.

The truth is that when we become "perfectly human," we become more open, more vulnerable, more apt to make and admit mistakes, more free. Perfection has to do with the ability to relate deeply and lovingly with others.

May our Creator take away our fears of spiritual growth.

September 16

A thousand years to you are like one day. . . , like a short hour in the night. . . . Remember how short my life is; remember that you created all of us mortal!
PSALMS 90:2; 89:47

To know that a thousand years to God is like one day is little comfort when we are living, bound to twenty-four-hour days, waiting and praying for changes in ourselves or in our living situations. And, like the psalmist, we want to pull at God's arm, reminding our Creator of how short our lives are. We do not have time to wait a thousand years. In fact, we do not want to wait even a day.

This impatience seems to be especially true for persons beginning Twelve-Step living. We forget that it took us years, sometimes most of a lifetime, to get into the mess we were in. We overlook the fact that all our bad habits and addictions developed over extended lengths of time. We become impatient with God, needing signs and proof that things are getting better. The sign that God often tries to give us first to make things better is patience.

May we receive God's gift of patience.

September 17

Don't be worried about those who prosper or those who succeed in their evil plans. PSALM 37:7B

The psalmist says that we do not need to envy people who are prospering while doing wrong. They will be punished. But what about those who are succeeding in their spiritual journey by doing what is right? A problem that can creep into a Twelve-Step group or even among friends or family members who are concerned with spiritual growth is the temptation to compare spiritual growth. We envy those who seem to be more successful, more serene, more insightful than we are. We sometimes find ourselves looking for faults in them or saying things to cut them down.

Envy in any form is a shortcoming that needs to be removed. We do not need to compare ourselves with others. We need not think that another's well-being somehow indicates our lack of well-being. We can glory in the serenity of others without feeling that their success diminishes our own, as if somehow there is a limited amount of serenity to go around and if someone else gets it, we might not. The antidote to envy is humility and a sense of humor about ourselves.

May the Creator of all give us joy in the successes of others.

September 18

Remind me each morning of your constant love, for I put my trust in you. My prayers go up to you, let me know the road I must take. PSALM 143:8

The psalmist reflects two deeply human needs, two things we want from God: clear signs of God's love and unmistakable direction for our lives. We become exceedingly frustrated when we feel we do not have these things. "If only I could be sure God cares for me." "If God would just point me in the right direction."

But the verse is not a statement of frustration or empty hope. The psalmist has also taken action, made some decisions, entered into a relationship. He says that he has put his trust in God and that he prays.

Our eyes cannot see signs of our Creator's love until we have taken the first steps to move into a trust relationship with God. Neither can we ever be directed in our lives unless we take the time to pray, to talk to God and listen to what God has to say. God's love is constant; our Comforter's arms are always open. Our task is to turn toward those arms, opening ourselves up to the signs of God's love, signs that can give us a sense of direction for our lives.

May we discover the love and guidance of God in our lives.

September 19

If your axe is dull and you don't sharpen it, you have to work harder to use it. It is smarter to plan ahead.
ECCLESIASTES 10:10

This advice seems so obvious, and yet in our daily lives we all find ourselves trying to cut meat with a dull knife, material with a dull pair of scissors, grass with a dull mower.

But more problematic are the emotional and spiritual skills that we allow to get dull. We work on being good to ourselves and noting all our strengths for a time and then slide back into our old habits. We learn to say "no" and to set our own boundaries, but before we know it, we are once again in the position of being drained by those we love. We learn to turn problems over to God, and our lives become so much better, but gradually we take the problems back.

Like an axe, our emotional or spiritual skills can get dull from use unless we take time to sharpen or clean them. Or they can get dull from disuse, from lying around getting rusty. All the spiritual and emotional skills we learn are like tools. They need to be kept in good working order.

May God help us keep our "tools" in good working order.

September 20

People with a hot temper do foolish things; wiser people remain calm. PROVERBS 14:17

Those of us with tempers can certainly agree with the writer of this proverb that we do foolish things. But even those of us for whom an uncontrollable temper is not a problem find there are times when we say or do spontaneous, hurtful things. For instance, we might say in exasperation, "Can't you ever do anything right." Such outbursts can cause spiritual, mental, emotional, and sometimes physical damage to those we love.

As we make a list of all those whom we have hurt, we need to take full responsibility for our thoughtless outbursts, recognizing that they have worked to diminish others' self-image and trust in our love. If the others are our children, such outbursts make it difficult for them to imagine a God who radiates steady love and will not, in fury, punish them. We cannot undo or repair the damage we may have done to others, but we can confess to them how we have wronged them and work very hard with our Creator's help to change our behavior.

May God create in us a calm mind and heart.

September 21

The Lord gave us mind and conscience; we cannot hide from ourselves. PROVERBS 20:27

Our best allies as we set out to make amends to those we have hurt are our minds and our consciences. We can trust our consciences to nag us, forcing us to surface and think about times we have hurt others. Sometimes those hurts were delivered through things we said or did; other times they were the result of our inaction, our inattention, our self-absorption.

First on our list should be those persons who are currently a part of our lives – our family, friends, co-workers. These are the persons who will continue to be hurt until we apologize and change our behavior.

The second group on our list should be those persons in our past with whom we have lost contact. This may include employers we have wronged, lost friends, strangers who were hurt by our behavior.

Finally, there are those for whom we can never make direct amends because they are dead or inaccessible. Our indirect amends to them are our new, responsible lives.

May our God use our minds and our consciences as we set about making amends.

September 22

You have done everything you have promised; Lord, your love is eternal. Complete the work that you have begun. PSALM 138:8

The woman clung to this prayer during the long, dark months of crisis when her whole life was infected and her relationships poisoned. It seemed as if major surgery was being performed without anesthesia on her spirit, and all she could feel was pain.

But she kept praying, "God, please complete the work you have begun." The healing process was slow and not altogether steady, but gradually the infection subsided and the wounds began to mend.

But even after she had moved past this critical point in her life, she kept praying this prayer as a part of her daily meditation. She knew that she would never be completely whole. She would always need her Creator working in her life, working to help her hold onto hope and to love herself and others. She would need to trust God when the path ahead was dark. She had learned through her suffering that God was at work in her life. Now she prayed that God would keep working every day.

May our Creator complete the work begun in us.

September 23

If I had ignored my sins, the Lord would not have listened to me. PSALM 66:18

One of the most important words in the Tenth Step is the simple word *when*, "when we are wrong. . . ." Had the word been *if*, there would have been the implication that perfection is possible. But, the word *when* helps us relax. Perfection will never be ours. We will always be wrong some of the time, just as we will be right some of the time. We can assume that. Making mistakes does not make us less acceptable or less loveable people.

God does not expect us to be perfect, but God does expect us to acknowledge those times when we are wrong. By ignoring our wrongdoing, we risk losing communication with the Source of our life. We also risk falling back into old, destructive patterns of thought and behavior that will erode our self-esteem and our relationships.

We learn from the Tenth Step what to do when we are wrong – promptly admit it to ourselves, to the person we have wronged, and to God; make what amends we can; and then move on.

May the Source of all life make of our mistakes an opportunity for growth.

September 24

When I see the wicked breaking your law, I am filled with anger. PSALM 119:53

If anger is always a secondary emotion, what might have been going on in the writer of this verse as a primary emotion? We like to think that he was filled with righteous indignation simply because of the pain he felt – pain rooted in his deep love for God – when he saw God's law being broken.

Our own motivations are often more complicated. When we see others behaving in ways that conflict with our interpretation of God's word, we sometimes are envious first, and then angry. Or we might be threatened first. Our whole value system is called into question, and we respond with anger. If the people are family members or friends, we feel personally rejected and our value system seems repudiated. Anger quickly follows.

Anger is always a red flag. When it goes up, we need to stop, look at ourselves, and listen to our inner voices. What is really going on? What did I feel first? What can I do to heal the emotion that produced the anger?

May God help us as we struggle with our anger.

September 25

You have given humans dominion over the works of your hands; you have put all things under their feet.
PSALM 8:6

Persons concerned with the exploitation and rapid deterioration of the planet's ecosystems are critical of the idea that somehow humans are superior to and separate from all other parts of the created order. They feel this belief gives to persons so inclined license to exploit, plunder, and destroy the earth's resources for their own benefit with little thought of long-term effects.

Spiritual renewal clearly involves being reconnected with God, self, and others. But it also involves reconnection with the whole created order – seeing ourselves as an integral part of a very complicated system that needs constant care and tending. According to our creation stories, we are responsible for the welfare of the earth. This involves living with love and respect for the created order and cherishing it as a sacred trust passed from one generation to the next.

May we celebrate our connection to all that God has created.

September 26

How I love to do your will, my God! I keep your teaching in my heart. PSALM 40:8

The art of meditation involves stilling the "mind chatter" that goes on in our brains all the time, quieting it so that we can hear the important voices. There are many ways of doing this. For some, it helps to take a short slogan or prayer and say it over and over again.

Others find it helpful to read a short section of the Bible two or three times (for instance, one of the psalms), focus on it, reflect on it and it only. Question it. What is God telling me?

When we are sure that the "mind chatter" has been stilled and our focus is on the words, we can relax and let our minds begin to float. It is at this point that our Creator can speak to us, leading our thoughts or images to the places they need to go, guiding us gently toward truth, showing us what is necessary for this day. God will not give us a lifetime task or a ten-year plan. Because our Helper wants us to keep our focus on the day, the guidance we receive will be just for today. And that is enough.

May God guide and lead us this day.

September 27

I am not concerned with great matters or with subjects too difficult for me. PSALM 131:1B

The man sat off in a corner, feeling out of place and very much wishing he had not come. It seemed absurd that attending such a meeting could help anyone. The leader had opened the meeting and introduced the topic – the Eleventh Step. Hardly had she begun talking when a woman broke in, "This is the worst Step for me. I can't help but wonder if prayer makes any difference. . . ." She forcefully presented her questions, using her own life story to justify her doubt. Then each person jumped in to give her or his bit of "proof" on one side or the other. No one's mind was changed, and the man went away unhelped.

Many people spend their whole lives hiding behind their questions, letting their doubt block them from growth. While questions are valid and while doubt is a part of the human struggle, we must let go of the need for conclusive proof in order to walk the spiritual journey. If we act as if God were real and involved in our lives, we will discover it is true.

May the Source of our being help us let go of our needs for proof.

September 28

God forgives all my sins and heals all my diseases . . . filling my life with good things, so that I stay young and strong like an eagle. PSALM 103:3, 5

What an incredible thing it is to know that God is working for us, forgiving our sins, healing our diseases of body and spirit, and filling our lives with good things. The psalmist makes it clear what God wants for us – to stay young, young in body and mind, and to be strong like an eagle.

We can learn much about strength from the image of an eagle. While the wings of an eagle are powerful, the eagle learns early to use that power to reach the high air currents. Then the eagle can soar effortlessly with a panoramic view of the world below.

How much easier our lives would be if we could quit expending our limited strength battling the surface winds – those gusts of attachment or despair, envy or anger, greed or pride – and set our sights on higher things. Then the current of God's Spirit could pick us up, and we would soar.

May God lift us on the current of love and let us soar.

September 29

Come and listen, all who honor God, and I will tell you what God has done for me. PSALM 66:16

Sharing the message of God's love and forgiveness is a complicated process of communication that depends both on teller and listener. We cannot, finally, determine whether our listeners will accept what we offer, but our attitude toward them will greatly affect the likelihood of our being able to share.

We must begin with a deeply imbedded belief that we cannot change another, nor should we try. Our sharing is not for the other, not to fix the other, not to make of the other a convert to our brand of spirituality. Our message must have no stated or implied shoulds or shouldn'ts, no attempts at control, no follow-up to see if we have been effective in getting our message across. Neither should it spring out of our desire to impress the other.

We simply share our story when it seems appropriate, telling what our Creator has done for us. We do it because we are overflowing with gratitude to God. Any other motivation will distort the message.

May God fill us to overflowing with gratitude.

September 30

Light shines in the darkness for good people, for those who are merciful, kind, and just. PSALM 112:4

The image of darkness is used in the Scriptures for those times of loss, grief, despair, doubt, or tragedy – those times when the world feels like a very cruel place, and our souls sink into night. When others are going through such times, we raise our fists to God, "How could you let this happen to such a good person?" When our time comes, we hardly have the strength to question God.

Yet the psalmist assures us that for those of us involved in walking a spiritual path, the darkness will never be complete. There will always be a light somewhere – an unexpected contact with a loved one, an unsolicited gift of time or material possessions, an invitation, a caring letter or phone call.

When others are going through the darkness of the soul, we can help to assure them of God's love by being a small light in their dark world. When we reflect back on our dark times, our faith can be strengthened by realizing that God was touching us through small beams of light.

May we be God's light shining in the darkness.

October

October 1

Steadfast love and faithfulness will meet; righteousness and peace will embrace. PSALM 85:10

Finally it will all come together, this prophetic statement tells us. The two qualities of God, steadfast love and righteousness, will meet and embrace those two qualities God most wants for us – faithfulness and peace.

For those of us struggling to walk a spiritual path, it does not really matter, ultimately, what choices we make. God with infinite love will find a way to give us what we need – regardless of what we choose and what we give up. In the end it will make little difference which paths we decide to walk. Our Creator, who loves us all, will find a way to bring us together. Righteousness will embrace peace. We will be met with love and kissed by mercy. Our lives will be made right, and our hearts will finally be filled with the serenity we have longed for with infinite yearning.

Our daily lives are affected for good or ill by our day-to-day choices, but in the end it does not matter. God's love will embrace us all.

May we find hope and peace in the promises of our Creator.

October 2

In times of trouble I pray to the Lord; all night long I lift my hands in prayer, but I cannot find comfort. When I think of God, I sigh; when I meditate, I feel discouraged. PSALM 77:2-3

The psalmist begins his lament describing a time of spiritual night when prayer and meditation not only do not help, they make him more discouraged. When he needed God most, God was silent. Then the psalmist fills the psalm with questions – all of the "why" questions that plague each of us during times of trouble.

One of the most important tasks of the spiritual network of which we are all a part is to support each other prayerfully through these times of doubt and despair. The "why?" questions have no answers, but we must give each other permission and encouragement to ask them. The despair cannot be prayed away by the person plunged into darkness, but the community can uphold that person in prayer. When God seems most absent in the life of a friend, our love, prayers, and support are the presence of God.

May we be a part of God's spiritual network, helping others.

October 3

Everything leads to weariness — a weariness too great for words. Our eyes can never see enough to be satisfied; our ears can never hear enough. ECCLESIASTES 1:8

The writer speaks for all of us who have struggled with depression, who are restless or bored, whose hearts weep with hopelessness, whose lives seem unfulfilled.

Depression can be a disease of the body for which medical help is needed, or it can signal a dis-ease of the spirit, a problem that can be handled only through spiritual means.

We sometimes cannot understand why things never seem to work out in our professional or personal lives. We do everything we can to make our lives better but to no avail. Finally we give up and fall into despair. It often takes many failures, many rejections, before we finally realize that our lives are not in our control. Then we are ready to begin our spiritual journey, a walk of faith in which we will gradually learn that our lives are in much stronger, wiser hands than our own. Our lives are in God's hands.

May God's strong hands hold us and guide us this day.

October 4

I will think about all that you have done; I will meditate on all your mighty acts. PSALM 77:12

This plan is the psalmist's response to a time of great discouragement and questioning of God's power and love. He has decided to stop thinking about what God has not done and begin thinking about what the Creator *has* done. In addition, he has plans to stop meditating on all of his own problems and, rather, meditate on God's mighty acts: creation and deliverance from bondage.

The relationship between our feelings and our thoughts is complicated, but it is sometimes possible to alter the way we feel by consciously changing the way we think. For instance, letting our thoughts dwell on all our own troubles or all the ways that God or others have failed us only makes our despair worse. We can choose to think about something else, perhaps focusing on all that is good in our lives or on the needs of others. Or, like the psalmist, we can look at the created order and know that God is powerful.

Our moods do not need to control us. By changing what we can – the way we think – we can work for our own well-being.

May our Creator help us overcome feelings of despondency.

October 5

All my bones can be seen. My enemies look at me and stare. PSALM 22:17

The stark image the psalmist creates is of one who is publicly vulnerable, naked before the world – without even skin. It is the picture of one who has hit bottom and lost all control, who is powerless and alone. How odd it would seem to us if this person suddenly said, "My life is OK – better than a lot of other people's. I may have a few problems, but I can handle them." We would think he was crazy if he tried to bandage his own gaping wounds, cover his unprotected bones, or deny the pain of his own situation.

And yet we often underestimate or try to minimize the problems in our own lives – those problems within ourselves, in our relationships, and in our work. If we can say that it is not so bad, that others are worse off, then we never have to admit our powerlessness, and we can keep trying to control things ourselves.

To have our sanity restored, we must give up our attempts to do what we know is impossible and then come to believe that a power greater than ourselves can restore our wholeness, health, and serenity.

May God continue restoring our emotional and spiritual health.

October 6

God remembered that they were only but flesh, a passing breath that does not return. PSALM 78:39

The seriousness with which we take our lives must sometimes amuse and other times sadden God. Our minds see through a microscope, magnifying the smallest event or the most insignificant comment all out of proportion.

If we think about it, we know how much emotional energy we have wasted fearing events that never happened or, if they did happen, turned out to be more helpful than hurtful. We know how foolish most of our anger, envy, and resentment was. But still, it is hard to apply that lesson to the present. And so we fuss and stew, increasing the magnification of our mental microscope rather than decreasing it.

But God remembers that we are mortal beings, here today and gone tomorrow. Our Creator knows that today is important to us, and that little things do make a difference. So God looks upon our foolishness with kindness and does whatever is possible to make our days more pleasant — which might include helping us learn to chuckle at ourselves.

May God give us a sense of proportion and humor about our lives.

October 7

God sets the time for silence and the time for talk.
ECCLESIASTES 3:7B

The words of her father, "There is a time and a place for everything," came to the woman as she left her small group meeting. Once again she had dominated the discussion, talking obsessively about her problems, wanting advice, needing approval, seeking answers. As the meeting wore on, she had felt the group, which had once been intensely interested in her life, pulling away from her. Were they frustrated? Bored? Did they no longer care about her? It had seemed so right, at first, to come and talk, but now. . . ?

The woman walked into the night thinking about everything she had said and everything she had heard. Gradually, the voices clamoring in her mind faded to a whisper. And then the silence she had always feared pressed in upon her, seeping into her soul. But, much to her surprise, rather than feeling empty and void, she felt filled. God had come in the silence, giving her a sense of well-being she had never known.

May the Source of life work in our lives through silence.

October 8

God will put angels in charge of you to protect you wherever you go. They will hold you up with their hands to keep you from hurting your feet on the stones. Psalm 91: 11-12

For her fifth birthday, she had been given a picture of a small boy and girl walking through a woods with a guardian angel behind them. The picture hung on her bedroom wall for years, its image soaking deep into her soul.

Now, as an adult, even though she no longer believed in the existence of angels, during those times when she felt most like a child (vulnerable, frightened, and weak) the image would rise out of her unconscious. She could almost feel the hands of her guardian angel on her shoulders, guiding, protecting, and comforting her. It gave her a strong sense of divine presence in her life even though she could hardly have articulated the feeling rationally.

God's hope for us all is that we feel the support and strength of divine presence in our lives.

May we be given this day the awareness of divine presence.

October 9

If I take wing with the dawn to come to rest on the western horizon, even there your hand will be guiding me, your right hand will be holding me fast.
PSALM 139:9-10

While it is a wonderful comfort to feel the presence of God in our lives, the Scriptures tell us over and over again that God's presence is not dependent upon our feelings. The writer of Psalm 139 describes all of the places where we could go – even to the land of the dead – but nowhere would we be without God. We can trust that. God is with us.

How can that knowledge affect the way we live? Certainly it should mean that we do not have to live with worry and fear as our constant companions. They are inner adversaries, fighting against all that is good in us, all that is strong, all that is noble. Knowing that God is with us can give us the courage and strength to step out in trust, to take risks, to celebrate our gifts, to strive toward being all that our Creator knows we can be. Knowing God is with us can help us give freely of ourselves for the sake of others.

May we be filled with the strength that comes from knowing of God's presence.

October 10

I hear an unknown voice saying, "I took the burdens off your backs; I let you put down your loads of bricks." PSALM 81:6

"I never really believed in God," the voice was so soft the others could hardly hear him, "except that I always blamed God for all my troubles." He laughed a little. "That seems silly, now that I think about it. I must have believed all along. I just didn't believe that God was on my side.

"But something happened to me while I was in treatment. I can't explain it, exactly. My perspective changed. Instead of blaming God for all the bad, I began to see a pattern of good – still being alive, getting the treatment I needed, being touched by loving and caring people. Suddenly I realized that, in spite of all the mistakes I had made, God was giving me another chance. God was on my side."

The psalmist tells us that even when we do not know the voice of God, God is at work easing our burdens and giving us a better life.

May we recognize the work of our Helper in our lives.

October 11

Even my best friend, the one I trusted most, the one who shared my food, has turned against me. PSALM 41:9

The psalmist describes one of the most painful situations any of us has to face — trusting someone and having that person turn against us, betray us, hurt us. If this happened to us as children, particularly if the trusted person was a parent, the wound can be very deep, remaining infected well into adulthood.

Those of us who are victims of broken trust tend to cut others off. We have a hard time sharing real feelings. We long for intimacy but sabotage our own efforts. We assume that those we love now will treat us in the same way that we were treated when we were children. And, because we often get from people what we expect from them, people do let us down.

We wrong our friends when we set them up to treat us badly. We shortchange our close relationships when we allow old infections to spread. As we take our own inventory, we can try to determine where those old wounds are and begin working toward healing.

May our Comforter and Helper heal the wounds from our pasts.

October 12

You created every part of me; you put me together in my mother's womb. I praise you, for I am awesomely, wondrously made; your work is wonderful. I know it with all my heart. PSALM 139:13-14

The mother wondered why her pain and grief were so deep when she heard her son talk with such self-hate, expressing great dissatisfaction with his life. He complained of not being handsome enough or bright enough. He focused on all that he could not do and bemoaned his lack of self-esteem. It was very difficult for the mother not to feel she had failed. She longed for the satisfaction of knowing that the child she had raised felt good about himself.

When we are critical of ourselves, not only are we being critical of our parents, we are also criticizing God who put us together in our mother's womb and who loves us and is satisfied with us just as we are. The best gift we can give to God is satisfaction with and love for what God made — ourselves. We honor and praise God when we see in ourselves the wonder and creativity of our maker.

May God fill us with the wonder of our own uniqueness.

October 13

I said, "I am falling": but your constant love, O Lord, held me up. PSALM 94:18

The college senior sat in her counselor's office weeping with exhaustion, pouring out one story after another of all her friends who were in deep trouble and relying on her for help.

The counselor empathized. "When I am ready to jump into the deep waters with a friend who is flailing frantically about, I remember this. Most drowning people are helped more by being tossed a life preserver and encouraged by the voices of people on shore than by the heroic attempts of someone jumping in to save them." "But they need. . . ." The counselor smiled. "You think they need your help. But the help you are giving is robbing them of the dignity of helping themselves. And *you* are being drowned in the process. Let your love and respect for them hold them up as they struggle for shore."

May God help us assist others without hurting ourselves.

October 14

Happy are those whose sins are forgiven, whose wrongs are pardoned. PSALM 32:1

The child lay terrified in her bed, her dark room filled with ghosts. Where she had draped her bathrobe, a long-armed creature loomed, waiting to grab her. On the wall where a picture had hung, a dark presence threatened to swallow her. And, at the bottom of her bed, she felt an evil force stir, moving toward her, ready to destroy her. She screamed into the night.

Within seconds, her mother was at the door, turning on the light. The night vanished, the evil forces disappeared, and once again she was secure in her friendly room, her dog snuggling against her.

Doing a Fifth Step is like having God shine a light on even the darkest corners of our lives, those places where we store the old guilts that haunt us in the night, that keep us from living free and open lives. Once exposed to the Light, those guilts lose their power over us and vanish. God wants to forgive us, to free us from the ghosts of our past.

May the Source of all light shine a light into our darkest places.

October 15

Lord, you have examined me and you know me. You know everything I do; from far away you understand all my thoughts. PSALM 139:1-2

How odd it is to think that there is someone who knows us far better than we know ourselves. We know something about our actions, but we know little about what they do—whom they hurt, whom they help. But God knows. We know what we are thinking most of the time and what we are feeling some of the time, but we rarely understand why we are thinking or feeling that way. God not only knows, but understands.

That means that we are understandable. All of the weird quirks in our behavior, the surges of uncontrollable feeling, the fantasies or dreams, the self-destructive behaviors—all those things about ourselves that drive us crazy are understood by God. Not only does our Creator understand them, but God accepts and loves us just as we are. We can never be fully understood by our friends or even by ourselves, but that does not mean that we are not understandable. To God, what we are makes perfect sense.

May we bask in the awareness of our Creator's understanding of us.

October 16

Wash away my evil and make me clean from my sin!
PSALM 51:2

In one way the psalmist is talking about the Fifth Step experience of confession, which brings with it forgiveness. We admit the evil from our pasts, and God washes it away. But this could also be seen as a two-part process: having our evil washed away (something that happens and is complete) and the long process of God working in us to make us clean (the Sixth and Seventh Steps).

It is easy to become very impatient with the process, to want to be clean immediately. The very impatience with which we approach the Sixth and Seventh Steps is a defect which needs to be admitted and removed. To give it up means admitting that for the rest of our lives we will be working with God on ourselves. There is no easy fix or quick cure. The removal of one defect often sheds light on another hidden beneath it.

We can see the process as frustrating and never-ending, or we can see it as an exciting challenge. We *can* grow toward wholeness, and that is what God wants to help us do.

May God give us patience as we grow toward wholeness.

October 17

People with quick tempers cause a lot of quarreling and trouble. PROVERBS 29:22

All of us who have struggled with an uncontrollable temper know the problems it causes. Blowing up always makes the situation worse. And then we have to live with both the increased trouble and our own sense of failure for having lost control once again. A bad temper is a personality shortcoming that we need to ask God to remove.

But what about those of us who live or work with someone with a bad temper? While it is possible for that person to change, we cannot force the change. How can we learn to live constructively with a person with a destructive temper? The most important skill we need to learn is the ability to detach, to not get pulled into the storm, to respond with self-control and calm, even humor. It always "takes two to make a fight." By remaining calm in the face of an angry outburst, we can prevent the outburst from becoming a quarrel. And we can spare ourselves the emotional drain of becoming enmeshed in an irrational scene.

May our Helper give us calm and detachment in the face of anger.

October 18

If you repay good with evil, you will never get evil out of your house. PROVERBS 17:13

The goal that the writer sets before us is to create a home that is free from evil, a place of love and kindness where we can escape from the cares and pressures of the world and be nurtured and fed. He points out the importance of not repaying good with evil as one way to get evil out of the house.

More insidious than the temptation to repay good with evil, however, is the temptation to repay evil with evil. When someone does something that hurts us, our first impulse is to pay back, to punish, to get even. Our attempts at "justice" simply escalate the cycle of hurt. It keeps going around and around and never stops until someone says, "No, I will not be a part of this anymore."

At this point, there is hope that the level of "evil" in the house, if not eliminated, will certainly be lowered. Only then can the home become a place where good things happen between people who care about each other.

May our Deliverer free us of the desire to repay evil with evil.

October 19

I recognize my faults; I am always conscious of my sins. PSALM 51:3

Recognizing our faults and asking God to remove them is an ongoing process. One reason is that as we mature, what was at one time appropriate behavior may become a fault. It is not a fault for a baby to cry, demanding that someone meet her needs. But that is not appropriate behavior for an adult. We are responsible for meeting our own needs or finding mature ways of asking for help.

Early in our recovery, it is very important to keep our focus on ourselves—to always do what is best for us so that we can maintain our fragile hold on serenity and not get pulled back into our old behaviors. But as we grow toward health, that positive self-focus can turn into self-centeredness and a refusal to take into consideration the feelings or needs of others. Because we have changed and grown, this trait, which was once positive, has become negative, and we need to have it transformed.

Because we are human—imperfect, growing, changing—our Seventh-Step task is never complete.

May God help us in the on-going process of recognizing our shortcomings.

October 20

As far as the east is from the west, so far does God remove our sins from us. PSALM 103:12

The whole of Psalm 103 is a beautiful song describing the love of God. Each verse touches us in a different way, but all assure us that we have a God who is actively at work making our lives more rich and full.

For those of us who have struggled to improve ourselves, expending enormous amounts of energy trying to overcome our shortcomings, and who have found over and over again that our efforts are like trying to keep wasps in a box with no lid, verse 12 tells us there is another way. We need to step back and say to God, "Please get these wasps out of my life. I am so tired of trying to contain them. Not only am I not successful, but the harder I try, the more opportunities they have to sting me." When we step back, God is free to help, taking the wasps one by one and removing them as far away as "the east is from the west."

May we give God the freedom to help us.

October 21

If your ruler becomes angry with you, do not hand in your resignation; serious wrongs may be pardoned if you keep calm. ECCLESIASTES 10:4

The implication of this verse is that there are times when we all make mistakes, sometimes serious mistakes. We find ourselves in situations in which someone is very angry with us and the anger is legitimate – we have failed in our responsibilities.

The natural response is to want to escape the anger. One way we can do that is by quitting the job, getting out of the marriage, breaking the relationship. Or we might set up a defensive counterattack, using our own anger as a shield to protect us from arrows of anger shooting toward us.

Either response could end the relationship. The writer of Ecclesiastes suggests that the best thing we can do is to remain calm. This includes taking responsibility for our mistakes, accepting the consequences, and doing what we can to make amends. We may or may not be pardoned, but at least we have not made a bad situation worse by our response.

May our Helper give us the courage to accept responsibility for our mistakes.

October 22

The words of the wicked are murderous, but the words of the righteous rescue those who are threatened. PROVERBS 12:6

The importance of words can hardly be overstated. The writer of this proverb notes that some words can kill, while others rescue. Some words bring death, while other words bring life.

We have all likely been the objects of abusive language, from the cruel names hurled at us by other children to the thoughtless words spoken by our parents, from the put-downs by our loved ones or friends to the ridicule of teachers or employers.

The sad truth about being the object of abuse of any kind is that even though we know how destructive such abuse is, we often are unable to stop ourselves from passing it on to others. Sometimes we even become like an amplifying system, picking up abusive words and spewing them out on others even louder and stronger, making them even more hurtful.

An important part of our Eighth-Step work is remembering those whom we have hurt with our words.

May God guard our tongues from speaking hurtful words.

October 23

Discipline your children, and you can always be proud of them. They will never give you reason to be ashamed. PROVERBS 29:17

The word discipline is often understood to mean "punish" or "chastise," and so parents use this verse and others like it from Proverbs to legitimize their own need for forced control over their children.

But the meaning of the word is far more profound and has something to say about all our relationships. Discipline comes from the Latin word for learning, which means to grasp or apprehend. There is no control issue here, no power play. A disciple chooses to follow a master because somehow the master has communicated a value system the disciple comprehends and accepts. The children who finally give their parents reason to be proud are those who have been taught a value system by word and example and then have been given the freedom to test it and to choose. The best relationships are those in which neither party seeks to dominate the other. Simply being who we are gives others the chance to freely grasp and perhaps incorporate our values.

May our Creator bless us as we live out who we are.

October 24

Depending on an unreliable person in a crisis is like trying to chew with a loose tooth or walk with a crippled foot. PROVERBS 25:19

Many of us have had the unsettling experience of "depending on an unreliable person." That person may have been our parent or perhaps our spouse or employer. Whoever it was, our reaction to being let down time and time again is usually one of bitterness, resentment, and anger. We may even have concluded that it was our fault and thought less of ourselves because of the other person's inadequacy.

Our resentment is a failing for which we should make amends, but trying to make amends to such people can often lead to greater frustration. They may use our vulnerability to abuse us further or attempt to control us or manipulate us. If it is clear that these persons are still deeply enmeshed in their own dis-ease (for instance, a parent who is still a practicing alcoholic or a person consumed with anger and bitterness), we may need to concentrate on freeing ourselves of the resentment, but leave the efforts to heal the relationships for another time.

May God give us discernment as we set about making amends.

October 25

They pay me back evil for good, and I sink in despair.
PSALM 35:12

The response of the psalmist is so familiar. When others behave badly, when others hurt us when we have done nothing to deserve the hurt, when others lash out at us for no reason, we sink in despair. The injustice of it all is overwhelming. We wonder if we are not somehow to blame, and we allow the others' bad behavior to destroy our spirit.

Sometimes, we even take on guilt for bad behavior that is not directed at us, as if we are responsible for the whole world. We carry guilt for the wrongdoing of others in our family. We may even carry guilt for the wrongdoing of our government, our religious institutions, or our schools. We think we need to atone for all of humanity's wrongs, past and present.

The Twelve-Step program, and particularly the Tenth Step, helps us keep our focus on ourselves. We are responsible only for our own wrongdoing. We need not carry any more than that — and we are learning how to let go even of that.

May our Deliverer free us from guilt for the wrongdoing of others.

October 26

The sun will not hurt you during the day, nor the moon during the night. The Lord will protect you from all danger. PSALM 121:6–7A

We all know of the many ways the sun can hurt us. It can burn our skin, cause cancer, dehydrate us, harm our eyes, or give us sunstroke. It is clear that we need to be protected from the destructive power of the sun's rays.

But why did the psalmist include the moon as a source of danger? The moon is usually associated with soft light and romance. Recent studies, however, have confirmed what ancient peoples knew to be true: the moon holds a strange power over our moods. The words "looney" and "lunatic" come from the Latin word for moon. During times of full moon, there is a marked increase in the number of suicides, homicides, instances of physical abuse, and any number of other emotion-related problems.

We do need to be protected from craziness both in ourselves and in others. And God has promised to keep us safe.

May the Creator of all protect us from danger.

October 27

Never boast about tomorrow. You don't know what will happen between now and then. PROVERBS 27:1

Over and over again, in a variety of ways, the scriptures reflect the wisdom of living "one day at a time." "Futurizing," its opposite, comes in two packages. Either we assume life will get worse and therefore live in fear, or we assume it will get better and concentrate on all the improvements we will make in our lives, all that we will be able to acquire or do.

We have no idea what the future holds for us — either good or bad. Ann Lee, who founded the Shaker community, said, "Do all your work as if you had a thousand years to live, and as you would if you knew you must die tomorrow." In either case, the future holds no power over us. We focus on the day, doing the best we can do, being the best we can be. We unwrap each day as if it were a precious gift, treasuring the moment, and cherishing ourselves in that moment. And we look with fresh eyes on all those around us, carrying no baggage from the past or expectations for the future. As we learn to live one day at a time it becomes possible for us to accept ourselves and others.

May God help us live in the day.

October 28

Send me your light and truth; may they lead me and bring me back to Zion, your sacred hill, and to your Temple, where you live. PSALM 43:3

In very practical, concrete ways, the Tenth and Eleventh Steps are intertwined. It is often through our prayer and meditation that we become aware of the times we have failed to live lovingly or the attitudes we have that are fettering us. A part of our "mind chatter" is often rationalization, self-justification, or blaming others. It may also be "getting even" scenes, in which we play out the perfect squelch or the ultimate put-down. Or we may babble to ourselves words of self-pity: "Why can't I have what others have? Why do I have troubles they don't have?"

We need to still those voices through meditation before God can help us see them for what they are: barriers to our freedom, freedom to love and be loved. We need to silence those voices before we can hear the voice of God saying, "I love you. I accept you. You are in my strong hands."

May the voice of God fill us with light and truth.

October 29

The Lord is gracious and compassionate, slow to anger and abounding in kindness. PSALM 145:8

Genesis 1:27 tells us that God created humans in God's own image. Could that mean that we are like our Creator in the same way that a child is like a parent? We will never be the parent, but we do have the potential to model ourselves after the parent, to try to behave like the parent behaves.

That idea makes verses describing our Creator helpful not only in knowing what we can expect from God, but also in knowing what our potential is, what our goals can be, what God is eager to help us become.

The psalmist tells us that God is "gracious and compassionate, slow to anger and abounding in kindness." These four characteristics each set for us a wonderful goal. What would our lives be like if we could be gracious in all our actions, if we could set aside ill-will in favor of compassion, if we could react with calm, if our kindness could be constant, unaltered by the behavior or attitudes of others?

May our Creator help us strive toward these goals.

October 30

So all your loyal people should pray to you in times of need; when a great flood of trouble comes rushing in, it will not reach them. PSALM 32:6

It would be nice to think that, once we have mastered the Twelve Steps, our lives will be problem-free. But, of course, we never do master them. Even if we could, we would not be without great floods of trouble rushing in: sickness, accidents, all the other unmanageables of life. Our lives will always have difficult times. We will always have to struggle with our own worst enemy, ourselves. In that sense, nothing has changed because of our efforts toward spiritual recovery.

But, in a much more profound sense, everything has changed. As the psalmist says, the trouble will rush in, but it will not reach us. It will be there, but it will not destroy us. We will be like the children of Israel, crossing the Red Sea on dry land. Our trust in God, our focus on the day, and our willingness to work our spiritual program give our Deliverer the opportunity to hold back the flood of troubles and save us.

May our Deliverer keep our feet on dry land.

October 31

I am content and at peace. As a child lies quietly in its mother's arms, so my heart is quiet within me. PSALM 131:2

The first time the woman read this verse, she was going through a stage of personal turmoil in which she felt as if caffeine were being injected straight into her heart. She spent her fitful nights planning how she could make things better and her days trying desperately to carry out her plans. She wanted nothing more than to feel content, but she assumed she needed to fix her life first. So she hung onto her anxiety as if it were a towline that would pull her through her problems.

The irony is that frenetic activity born out of anxiety is rarely productive—and often counterproductive—like the flailing about of someone caught in quicksand. We need to learn that contentment is possible, and in fact most necessary, when there is trouble in our lives. The real movers of mountains in this world are those who walk steadily through their problems doing what they can do, content and at peace.

May our Comforter quiet our hearts and give us peace.

november

November 1

By the rivers of Babylon we sat down; there we wept when we remembered Zion. PSALM 137:1

The book of Lamentations tells us what the people of Judah were thinking and feeling as they wept in Babylon, slaves in a foreign land, their own cities and countryside ravaged. They painfully recalled all the mistakes they had made, the countless ways they had separated themselves from the protection of their God. God had finally let them pay the price for their actions and had given their enemies victory over them.

With nothing left of their former lives, the people of Judah could have become bitter and hateful toward God or concluded that there was no God. But in their emptiness and despair, they realized what had been impossible for them to see before. Finally God was all they had, and God's unfailing love and mercy still continued. All they could do was trust and wait to be rescued.

Deep in our own darkness, those weeping voices come to us, giving us hope.

May we learn to trust God in our times of darkness.

November 2

So life came to mean nothing to me, because everything in it had brought me nothing but trouble. It had all been useless; I had been chasing the wind. ECCLESIASTES 2:17

When we find our souls filled with frustration and rage over the uselessness of our lives, when all effort seems hopeless and all struggle in vain, when we yearn for purpose and meaning, then we know that we have not yet laid claim to our calling.

We all have been summoned to a vocation, a calling, a task in this world for which we are uniquely qualified. Sometimes that vocation is what we do to earn a living. Often it is not. The call is from God, who needs us to be passionately engaged with the world, working to bring healing and wholeness to all creation. Our call resonates deep within us, interweaving with our gifts and talents in a way that creatively empowers us. We have no road maps, no guides, only a call.

When we hear that call and respond with a hesitant but faithful yes, then rage and frustration fade, and hope can grow.

May we hear and respond to our calling.

November 3

I realized another thing, that in this world fast runners do not always win the races, and the brave do not always win the battles . . . and capable people do not always rise to high positions. Bad luck happens to everyone. ECCLESIASTES 9:11-12A

From national security to financial security, from employment security to domestic security, we all strive for security. We want to know that we are safe, that our futures are ensured. We cling to the symbols of security: military strength, insurance policies, pension plans, tenure, dead-bolt locks, handguns.

But security is a bogus concept. None of us is ever really secure. Bad things can happen to anyone, randomly and without warning.

How can we learn to live with that reality without always living timidly and fearfully? Accepting our powerlessness sets the stage for us to begin relying on God. God does not cause bad things to happen, nor does God always prevent them from happening, but God *does* promise to be with us during the bad times, holding our spirits secure.

May our Deliverer liberate us from fear and insecurity.

November 4

So then, you will get what you deserve, and your own actions will make you sick. PROVERBS 1:31

Wisdom (Sophia) is speaking in this verse, telling those who have never wanted her advice or correction that their own actions will make them sick. She reflects a truth that is obvious when we look at our own lives. When we make mistakes, we pay a price. When we behave foolishly, we suffer.

While this is obvious in relation to our own lives, we sometimes cannot see that it works in the lives of others. They behave badly and seem not to pay a price, and our sense of fairness or justice is shattered. We sometimes even think that it is our responsibility to make another pay. This is particularly true when what the other has done has caused us or those we love suffering. Our need to get even consumes us. We find it hard to trust that this person will get what he or she deserves.

We are never called to try to get even with others, but to try with God's help to love those who hurt us.

May God lift from us the desire to get even.

November 5

If you love money, you will never be satisfied; if you long to be rich, you will never get all you want.
ECCLESIASTES 5:10

When we ask God to restore our sanity, we admit that many of our attitudes and behaviors have been destructive to ourselves and others. One such behavior is taking our unhappiness or our boredom and sublimating it in a power greater than itself. These powers include the love of money, food, drugs, sex, status, relationships, self-pity, aggression, education, gambling, religion, music, sleep, work. . . .

The writer of Ecclesiastes tells us that if we love money, we will never be satisfied. Neither will we be satisfied by any of these other loves that divert us from the spiritual dis-ease that is at our core.

As we begin to recognize the inability of all our old attachments to satisfy us, their hold on us fades. We squarely face our real spiritual dis-ease, realizing that only the Source of all life can penetrate deeply into our selves and bring healing.

May the Source of our being give us serenity.

November 6

Like an evening shadow, I am about to vanish.
PSALM 109:23A

As twilight descends, the sharp, clear shadows of the day soften until finally all the world is a shadow, all the world is dark. And in that darkness, whatever it was that defined us, that gave us shape and form, that set us apart as individuals is gone. We have lost our vision, lost our direction. Indeed, we have lost our sense of ourselves.

Walking in darkness is very risky. We stumble and fall, we bump into things we cannot see, our friends are indistinguishable from our enemies, and we fear beasts lurking beside the road, waiting to attack us.

The prophet Isaiah tells us that "the people who walked in darkness have seen a great light." To see the great light is a gift given to those who not only are plunged into darkness, but who also have the courage to keep walking even when it is impossible to see where they are going. During our darkest moments, we live with hope that if we keep walking, we, too, will see the great light.

May the Source of light give us hope as we walk in the darkness.

November 7

The danger of death was all around me; the horrors of the grave closed in on me; I was filled with fear and anxiety. PSALM 116:3

The writers of Psalms and Proverbs use the image of death to describe much more than physical death. To feel the "grave closing in on me" is to be cut off from hope and love. It is to be cut off from God. The oppressive force of our addictions enslaves us, our unmet needs surround us, our anxieties, resentments, and angers cripple us. Being in "danger of death" is having our most important relationships at risk, often through the consequences of our own behavior.

Becoming dependent on God by taking the Third Step is directly opposite to being dependent on drugs, alcohol, sex, relationships, control, or any of the other things we can become dependent on. All other dependencies cut us off from love, sap us of strength, and rob us of hope. But becoming dependent on God is like plugging into the Source of power. We become alive, filled with light, empowered, strong.

May the Source of life be our highest power.

November 8

God helps those who are in trouble; and lifts those who have fallen. PSALM 145:14

The desperate college student called home. She had agreed some months earlier to run for president of an organization and had been elected. Now she recognized that she had made the choice to run for all the wrong reasons. She wanted the prestige and power of the position, and the recognition she would receive. But now that she had the job, she realized that she had neither the time nor the energy for the incredible amount of detail and busywork the position required. She felt no power, only enormous responsibility.

Her mother empathized. She had been in similar positions many times. "When I realize I have dug myself into another hole, I say to God, 'I made another mistake. I let the shouting of my ego block out my true calling.' Then I ask God to take my bad choice and somehow use it for good." She chuckled a bit. "Sometimes I think God must get very tired of bailing me out of the messes I get myself into, but somehow, when I turn it over, things always get better."

May we give God the chance to use our mistakes for good.

November 9

I lift up my hands to you in prayer; like dry ground, my soul is thirsty for you. PSALM 143:6

We all spend our lives feeling thirsty, but most of us never quite know what it is that will satisfy that thirst. We attach ourselves to thirst-quenching notions: more security, a better self-image, deeper intimacy, romance, more knowledge, food, power. Or we assume that we can get rid of the thirst by avoiding certain things: boredom, anger, rejection, commitment, vulnerability, being alone. The human spirit has an endless ability to find things, activities, or ideas to consume in an effort to quench the thirst that is common to us all.

These things are not bad in and of themselves. However, when we use them to avoid acknowledging the cause of our real thirst, when they begin consuming our attention, when we panic and become anxious if they are threatened, then we have lost our freedom. The yearning for God is our real thirst. Nothing but God can quench it.

May we open ourselves to God and be filled.

November 10

I am like a deaf person and cannot hear, like a dumb person and cannot speak. I am like a person who does not answer, because he cannot hear. PSALM 38:13-14

The psalmist is neither deaf nor dumb, but he has reached a time in his life when he is cut off from communication with others, unable to respond in normal ways because something inside is keeping him isolated. He is alienated and alone.

We are created to love and be loved, to listen and be listened to, to touch and be touched. If we find ourselves feeling cut off from others, either because we see ourselves as unworthy of their love or because we see them as unworthy of ours, it is time to take a hard look inside. Perhaps we are wallowing in self-pity, beating ourselves for mistakes, repressing anger or hurt, or judging and blaming others. Our Fourth-Step inventory can help us determine what traits we have allowed to turn into walls blocking us from others.

May our Creator help us tear down the walls blocking us from others.

November 11

There is no one on earth who does what is right all the time and never makes a mistake. ECCLESIASTES 7:20

While we may acknowledge the truth of this verse in our minds, still, we spend much time and energy looking for the perfect person, someone we can love unconditionally or respect completely, someone at whose feet we can sit or whose behavior we can predict. We look for this perfect person in our political or religious leaders, or we try to find the perfect lover or friend. We may even try to raise the perfect child. And then when we discover, as we inevitably do, that this person is very human and has made and will continue to make some bad mistakes, we are deeply disillusioned and angry, as if he or she has personally failed us.

The problem, of course, is in our need for the human embodiment of God and the expectations we place on those persons whom we decide should fulfill that need. The process of maturity and love involves releasing others from our expectations for their behavior.

May God free us from the expectations we place on others.

November 12

Gossip is so tasty—how we love to swallow it! PROVERBS 18:8

It is the tastiness of gossip that makes it so destructive. We hear something and think, "That may or may not be true, I will disregard it." But gossip has a sweetness that we cannot resist. We savor the information and then swallow and digest it, letting it become a part of us, affecting us in ways we cannot control. Gossip alters our attitudes and therefore our behavior toward both the person about whom we heard the news and the person who spread the news. Relationships are always changed because of gossip—and never for the better. Some gossip spreads information that is true. Other gossip is only partly true or altogether false, and it causes problems so insidious that it ranks along with murder, stealing, and adultery as one of the destructive human behaviors condemned in the Ten Commandments.

Sometimes support groups can become hotbeds of gossip disguised as concern. In all our relationships, gossip—both listening to it and passing it on—is something we need to avoid.

May our Deliverer help us avoid gossip.

November 13

Happy is the person whom the Lord does not accuse of doing wrong and who is free from all deceit. PSALM 32:2

Before we complete the process, we live in fear that honestly doing a Fourth and Fifth Step will fill us with self-loathing. We have spent years building up defenses and rationalizations for our needs and behavior so that we will accept ourselves. We have worked hard to create a public image that will give us the respect and love we crave. What will happen when all of that is stripped away?

What happens is that we gain a totally new perspective. We see ourselves as we are, free from all the protective layers we have wrapped ourselves in. We stand naked before God, before another person, and before ourselves. And even in our nakedness—or perhaps *especially* in our nakedness—we are beautiful, we are acceptable, we are loved. To see, accept, and love ourselves just as we are, frees us to love others just as they are. We move into a life of infinite potential.

May the Source of our being free us to love ourselves just as we are.

November 14

You will never succeed in life if you try to hide your sins. Confess them and give them up; then God will show mercy to you. PROVERBS 28:13

Humans are potentially the most cruel of all beings, capable of doing all manner of evil to each other. Civilization depends upon humans learning not to act on these hurtful impulses.

When we were taught as children the difference between good and bad behavior, and the consequences of each, we began the struggle to resist the cruel impulses within. As adults, most often we repress them, and when they do pop out, we try to conceal the evidence of our badness. We have all ended up with a dark basement filled with monsters that keep growing and pounding at the door of our consciousness.

The psalmist tells us of a much better, easier way to deal with our own dark impulses – confess them and ask God to transform them. It is the difference between a life spent fighting inner monsters and a life spent opening the door and letting them out where they will be transformed by the light.

May the Source of light help us release our inner monsters.

November 15

My sacrifice is a humble spirit, O God; you will not reject a humble and repentant heart. PSALM 51:17

Humility is, in part, the admission that we do not know what is best for us or for others. As we seek to be ready to have God change us, we need to give up the notion that we can dictate either the nature of the change, or the process by which it is accomplished. It is a frightening act of faith to say to God, "I want to be different. You decide what should be different and how to bring about that change." We fear the defects we are willing to give up will not be the ones God sets out to remove first. We fear the pain that may be involved in the process of change. We fear that others will reject us if we become *too* different from the way we were.

Being "entirely ready" brings us back to the Third Step—turning our lives and wills over to God. Now, in the Sixth Step, we are turning over to God the right to change us in whatever way God chooses. And we can begin by turning over to God the fear we feel, asking for trust instead.

May our hearts be filled with humble trust in God's goodness.

November 16

Anger is cruel and destructive, but it is nothing compared to jealousy. PROVERBS 27:4

The word *jealous* at one time meant the same thing as the word *zealous,* but in time *jealous* came to mean a negative use of extreme passion or enthusiasm. *Zealous* has a more positive connotation. Anger is clearly destructive, but it can burst and be gone, whereas jealousy is an ongoing condition of intense possessiveness, passionate envy, or extreme resentment. Jealousy takes hotspots—normal problems in human interaction—and fans them until they are burning out of control. It lends emotional energy to all those forces within us that would hurt others and cut us off from them.

But even more destructive is jealousy's power to burn us out from the inside. It destroys our sense of our own uniqueness and calling, it shatters our self-image, and it erodes our self-confidence. And jealousy is insidious, creeping in when we least expect it.

Praying for deliverance from jealousy is a daily task.

May our Deliverer free us from jealousy's destructive power.

November 17

Too much honey is bad for you, and so is trying to win too much praise. PROVERBS 25:27

One of the common human addictions is the need for affirmation or praise. Affirmation, like honey, is a good thing. It helps us grow and mature. But there are two symptoms that indicate when our need for affirmation has crossed over into an addiction. The first symptom is when we lose our freedom to be who we are, when we struggle and behave in ways not authentic to our own calling in order to get praise from others.

The second symptom is when we set people up to affirm us, and then, when they do not take the bait, become hurt and angry, blaming them for being insensitive to our needs.

If we recognize either of these symptoms in ourselves, then we know that we have lost the ability to give and receive affirmation as a free gift with no strings. Our addiction is controlling our behavior and adversely affecting our relationships. It is time to admit our powerlessness and turn our need for affirmation over to God.

May God free us from the addictive need for affirmation.

November 18

They grow stronger as they go; they will see the God of gods on Zion. PSALM 84:7

In the Seventh Step, we ask God to remove our shortcomings. But whenever we remove anything without replacing it with something else, we create a vacuum into which something will flow. We have little control over what will rush into our spiritual vacuums. Often what rushes in is a shortcoming worse than the one removed.

As we work on having our shortcomings removed, an important part of our prayer is to ask God to fill us with a positive quality to replace the negative one. We pray that God will remove our short temper and fill us with tolerance and patience. We pray that God will remove our obsession with externals and fill us with delight in the internal. We pray that God will remove our disorganization and fill us with an appropriate sense of order and priorities.

As our shortcomings are removed, and we receive and integrate our new positive traits, we become stronger and stronger.

May God help us grow stronger as we journey.

November 19

When their [wicked] rulers are thrown down from rocky cliffs, the people will admit that my words were true. PSALM 141:6

How frustrating it must be for God that we recognize the truth of what God says only when we see our enemies get what we think they deserve. The human need for revenge (cloaked, usually, as a desire for justice) is so great that we often hang our belief in God on whether or not we see clear indications that those who have hurt us or others have been made to suffer.

The irony of this is that we also hang our belief in God on clear indications of God's mercy, providence, and love toward us and on God's willingness to forgive and not punish us. In other words, we have a double standard—justice for those who have hurt us and mercy for ourselves and those we love.

Our Creator is a God of both mercy and justice. But more important, God is love. We can only trust that God's love for us and for others will undergird both mercy and justice.

May we be filled with trust in God's love for us and others.

November 20

Lord, place a guard at my mouth, a sentry at the door of my lips. PSALM 141:3

We all from time to time, perhaps more often than we like to admit, let ill-advised words slip out of our mouths. But if we carefully control our words by turning on our inner editor and saying nothing that has not been carefully polished, we lose our spontaneity and freedom, and we seem remote and rigid. That very remoteness distances us from others, making us unable to enter into deep, meaningful relationships.

As we ask God to remove our shortcomings, the prayer of this psalmist might be appropriate. By daily turning our words over to God and letting go of our need to carefully edit our speech, we can live with the kind of abandon that comes from trusting that God will guard our mouths. We cannot know for sure which words will hurt and which will heal, but we can ask God to act as a sentry, letting out only those words that communicate honesty tempered by kindness, sincerity wrapped in acceptance, and hope undergirded by patience.

May God place a sentry at the door of our lips.

November 21

Smiling faces make you happy, and good news makes you feel better. PROVERBS 15:30

It is infinitely easier living with persons who are good-natured and content, happy with themselves and with their lives, than it is to live with those who are depressed or consumed with their own physical or emotional ailments. Before we began working on our spiritual recovery, the persons we love were likely touched by a moody, morose, self-centered, unpredictable person. And they have been hurt. Even if our poor emotional and spiritual health was not our fault, still it has greatly affected the people who love us.

A part of our amends to those persons would be to do whatever we can to open ourselves to the gift of serenity. If we are more serene, their experience of us will be more uplifting. We also need to accept them and love them for what they are—people who have been scarred by our dysfunction, people we cannot change or fix, only love. Even if the negative effects of our behavior are not apparent, still we need to be willing to make amends to all whom we have hurt.

May our Creator give us serene and content spirits.

November 22

The Lord sets prisoners free and gives sight to the blind. God lifts those who have fallen, and loves righteous people. PSALM 146:8

We sometimes feel as if we are prisoners of our pasts, locked into a cell of guilt, shame, and broken relationships that we have built for ourselves with our negative, willful behaviors and attitudes. Through the first nine Steps of the Twelve-Step program, God has been at work releasing us from our pasts. When we admit our powerlessness and put our lives in the hands of our Deliverer, we are on our way. Next, by taking a hard look at ourselves, admitting our wrongs, and asking God to remove our shortcomings, we have allowed God to transform us. Then, by consciously and directly making amends to all whom we have hurt, we have taken a significant step toward freedom from the bondage of our pasts.

Finally we are free to move forward. We have accepted what we could not change and changed what we could. It is time to concentrate on the present, living in the moment, moving forward into a new day.

May our Deliverer set us free from the bondage of our pasts.

November 23

We feast on the abundant food you provide; you let us drink from the river of your goodness. PSALM 36:8

Our bodies go through fifteen or twenty years of rapid growth, during which time it is important that they receive abundant nutrition for healthy development. After these years, our bodies only need maintenance nutrition. Our spirits are different. They never stop growing, never stop changing, are always developing in new and exciting ways. Because of that, our spirits need to be nurtured and fed nutritious food throughout our whole lives, or we will suffer from spiritual malnutrition.

That food can come to us privately through our reading of Scripture and other inspirational literature, and through meditation and prayer. It can also come to us through worship services or small groups that focus on spiritual renewal. Another source of spiritual food is the giving and receiving of loving acts.

The Tenth and Eleventh Steps help us keep our focus on the day, as we ask for and receive what we need to keep our spirits thriving.

May the Source of life provide us with abundant spiritual nutrition.

November 24

To you alone, O Lord, to you alone, and not to us, must glory be given because of your constant love and faithfulness. PSALM 115:1

The "us" referred to by the psalmist was the people of Israel. He was cautioning the people to remember that it was God who helped and protected them, not the national leaders nor the armies nor the priests of Aaron. The psalmist may have been responding to a celebration in which the people were congratulating themselves on a victory.

It is very important to express appreciation and gratitude to institutions or groups that help us — our governments, religious institutions, small groups, families, and friends. But it is more important to see these hands that help us as extensions of God's hands. These hands have many shapes and sizes and colors and work in ways we can hardly imagine. God comes to us in all the positive connections we experience.

In fact, our hands are also God's hands whenever they bring love and caring, kindness and nurturing, to another.

May we see God at work in the hands of those who help us.

November 25

Keep me from wanting to do wrong and from joining evil people in their wickedness. PSALM 141:4

One of the wonderful gifts that comes to people who have been struggling with an addiction is the point when, for no particular reason, they suddenly find themselves free from the desire for that substance. Sometimes this freedom is what begins the sober life. But most often it comes much later, after years of "working the program," trying to live a sober life in spite of an almost overwhelming desire for the addictive substance.

We all live with a variety of addictions or attachments that bind us to people, to things, or to ideas. While the objects of our attachments may or may not be harmful, in and of themselves, the attachments *themselves* are always harmful. Being released from the desire for the objects of our attachments gives us the freedom to choose all that is good. It is as if the chains that have kept us bound are broken, and we are free to enjoy our passions, love with abandon, and focus our attentions on our deepest yearning: to be closer to the Source of all love.

May our Deliverer free us from our attachments.

November 26

I pray to you, O Lord; you hear my voice in the morning; at sunrise I offer my prayer and wait for your answer. PSALM 5:3

Usually we think of prayer in certain ways—as rote prayer (table prayers, bedtime prayers, liturgical prayers) or as free prayer where we use our own words to talk to God. But prayer is much more than that.

Prayer is a connection to God. Think of the variety of meaningful connections we have with those we love: a brief touch in a crowded room, a glance, long hours of talking or listening or holding, acting in ways that show our love, expressing ourselves in song or poetry, telling secrets, having fun.

Prayer is our way of connecting with God whom we love, and it can happen in all of the same ways that we connect with others whom we love. It can take an hour or an instant, it can be a song or a sigh, it can happen at set times during the day or any time at all. Prayer is our way of keeping in touch with someone we love very much.

May we find delight in our prayer lives.

November 27

You are my God; teach me to do your will. Be good to me, and guide me on a safe path. PSALM 143:10

What is it that makes a path safe? According to biblical imagery, a safe path is a path through open spaces where hidden, unexpected enemies cannot overcome us. The path may be uphill or downhill, over rocky ground or through green meadows. We may need to wade through raging waters, or we may find bridges to make our crossings easier. On a safe path, we can still trip over our own feet or walk mindlessly into a tree. But on a safe path those enemies, both within and without, who seek to destroy us cannot get close enough to attack without our seeing them and being able to find shelter.

When we ask God to guide us on a safe path, what we may really have in mind is an easy path. The reality of existence on this earth is that no path is easy. No one escapes the troubles and pain common to all humanity. However, some paths are safer than others. And so we ask God to guide us on a safe path.

May we follow our Guide on a safe path.

November 28

Your knowledge of me is too deep; it is beyond my understanding. PSALM 139:6

Our prayer life, indeed our whole life, changes dramatically when it finally penetrates into the core of our being that God knows us far better than we know ourselves and that God is for us — for our well-being, for our health, for our happiness. The notion that we know what is best for ourselves vanishes. The idea that we can determine what God should do for others disappears. The assumption that God needs our insights and arguments in order to take action evaporates.

When we know that God is intimately concerned about us, our prayers become quiet, sometimes wordless. We enter God's presence and wait for a nudge, look for a signal, listen for the whisper of an idea. God may be moving us toward a person who will help us through a particularly bad time. Or God may need us to help someone else, and in so doing, help ourselves. We are a part of a network of spiritual journeyers, waiting for the whisper of God, who is *for* all of us.

May we feel the gentle nudge or hear the whisper of God.

November 29

If they fall, they will not stay down, because the Lord will help them up. PSALM 37:24

When we come to the Twelfth Step in our spiritual recovery, we are not at the end of the road but at the beginning of a lifelong spiritual journey. This is a journey during which we will continue to grow toward wholeness, increase in love, and deepen our serenity.

But we will also trip and fall as we encounter new or old obstacles along the path. We may be walking confidently along, enjoying the view, breathing deeply the fresh air of life, and fail to notice a rock in our path. Suddenly we find ourselves flat on our faces. It is a familiar position. We have been there before. But now we know that we do not need to stay there. The same God who has lifted us up countless times is still with us and will lift us up again, even as a loving parent will lend a hand to a toddler whose legs do not always remain steady. We need to back up, focus on Steps Ten and Eleven, and let God, once again, work to create in us a new self.

May we live free from the fear of falling.

November 30

Lord, I have given up my pride and turned away from my arrogance. PSALM 131:1a

It is said that when we are young we want to change the world. As we mature, our vision fades a bit, and we focus our attention on changing our community or our family. Finally, it hits us that our biggest problem is changing ourselves. This process is usually seen in negative terms as the loss of idealism or the diminishing of energy, or perhaps the onset of self-centeredness.

The notion that we can fix the world or anyone—even ourselves—is not idealism. It is arrogance, arrogance that is self-defeating. It sets up conflict and perpetuates a "winners and losers" world.

Our task is not to fix even ourselves, but to open ourselves up so that God can work through us, so that God's love for and acceptance of others can be seen in us. By our responsible lives and actions, we will give evidence of God's concern for the world.

May we be open to God's calling for us.

december

December 1

They are like trees planted in the house of the Lord, that flourish in the Temple of our God, that still bear fruit in old age and are always green and strong.
PSALM 92:13-14

The trees planted in the Temple area were given special attention, watered, nourished, and tended. As a result, they flourished, bearing fruit even in their old age.

The image is a beautiful one and gives us hope as we grow older. When we start to feel useless, unneeded, or unproductive, we begin to shrivel. Our spirits wither even as our bodies shrink. But the simple human act of tending to each other's needs, of showering each other with love and kindness, of nourishing each other with affirmation and encouragement can help us lead useful, productive lives until we die.

While such tending is important at every stage of life, it is especially important as we grow older, when losses have altered our image of ourselves and cut off our usual sources of nourishment. Knowing it is possible to find new ways to give and receive care gives us hope that we will flourish and bear good fruit all our lives.

May the Source of life nurture and sustain us all our days.

December 2

Turn to me, Lord, and be merciful to me, because I am lonely and weak. PSALM 25:16

When we are at the First Step in our spiritual recovery, we are like babies—weak, vulnerable, needing much gentle care. We have dropped all illusions that we can control many parts of our lives. We have admitted that we are powerless. We have faced ourselves and our lives as honestly as we can, and we recognize our nakedness, our helplessness, our dependence.

At this point, we must learn to be very good to ourselves. God wants us strong and filled with life. Our Creator wants us whole. If that is what God wants for us, then we can joyfully embrace those goals for ourselves. Gone are the days of self-deprecation, self-incrimination, and self-defeating behavior. Because the Source of life cares for us, we are allowed to care for ourselves. In fact, we are encouraged to do so. Because God loves us, we can freely love ourselves and do what is good for us. Because our Helper works for us, we can work for ourselves, taking our guidance from God and moving forward toward spiritual wholeness.

May the Source of our being fill us with the desire to care for ourselves.

December 3

I cry aloud to God; I cry aloud, and God hears me.
PSALM 77:1

The psalmist must have known that it is possible to cry in silence, or he would not have qualified his sentence with the word *aloud.* When we cry in silence, the tears flow inward, flooding our hearts, drowning our zest for life, suffocating our feelings. We build dams, but even as they hold the tears in, they block friends out. We become isolated in our grief, unresponsive both to our own needs and to the needs of others.

When the dam breaks and our tears rush out, flooding our pillows or the shoulder of a friend, we feel the pain and grief we had tried to avoid, and sometimes it is excruciating. But it is also the release we need before we can begin the healing process.

The ability to cry aloud is a gift from God to humans, a gift designed to help us through the losses and grief common to us all. It helps to restore us to wholeness. We need to allow ourselves and others to make full use of this gift.

May we know God's presence as we cry aloud.

December 4

I know that I will live to see the Lord's goodness in this present life. PSALM 27:13

The Second Step has been called the "Hope Step." It is the Step that clearly states that our lives can be better, that we can "see the Lord's goodness in this present life." Accepting this Step is like taking a turn in a dark tunnel. We are still in the tunnel. We still have a long way to go. But we do see a light at the end, and we accept the reality of that light.

It is at this point that the spiritual dimensions of our lives become a conscious journey. We have always been God's children. We have always been in God's care. But now we begin walking in a conscious awareness of that reality. We begin struggling with what that means for our lives. We begin growing in our understanding of the uniqueness of our own journey — we cannot walk someone else's path and neither can anyone else walk ours. But at the same time, we feel ourselves touched again and again by another, a touch that leaves both of us richer.

May our dark tunnels be brightened by the light of our Creator.

December 5

I am as useless as a discarded wineskin; yet I have not forgotten your commands. PSALM 119:83

On the way to visit her friend, the woman tried frantically to think of something she could say to cheer her up. But what do you say to a forty-year-old kindergarten teacher who is dying of cancer?

The hospice nurse opened the door and let the woman into the living room where her friend was propped up on the couch. The woman gasped. There was almost nothing left of her friend that she recognized except her smile. "Come and sit down," the friend encouraged. On the wall, the woman noticed a large, get-well poster on which all the children from her friend's class had made handprints and written their names.

"I keep it there so that each day, between naps, I can go through the class and pray for each child. I miss them, you know." A tear formed in her eye. "I can't teach them anymore, but I can pray for them."

The woman sat in silence as her friend cheered her up with stories of how she continued to find meaning in her life.

May our Comforter bless us with a sense of purpose for our lives.

December 6

The Lord guides people in the way they should go.
PSALM 37:23A

As they tied the blindfold over her eyes, they told her that this was going to be an experience that would help her understand faith. Unable to see a thing, she felt herself being led. At first she tried to orient herself. This must be the door. We must be walking down the hall. Soon we will reach the stairs. But nothing happened as she expected, and soon she realized that she had no idea where she was or where she was going. She was totally in the hands of her guide. Then she heard a voice saying, "Fall backwards." She panicked. It made no sense to do such a risky thing. How could she know that she would not land on the floor, hurt? But other voices joined the first urging her to trust. And so she let herself drop back and down. Many strong arms caught and held her.

Taking the Third Step is like this walk. We do not know where it will lead. We do not know that we will not be asked to do something risky. We take a chance. That is faith.

May the Source of life guide and protect us as we walk in faith.

December 7

How painful it is to the Lord when one of the faithful dies. PSALM 116:15

The funeral was for a man who had died of alcoholism, leaving behind a wife, three teenage children, and insurmountable debt. What could possibly be said in his behalf?

These words came ringing into the ears of those gathered to mourn. "I think God has a place of comfort and peace waiting for those who die of alcoholism. These are people who, at their core, are deeply and intensely spiritual, whose yearning for God leads them to a bottle and traps them inside, whose tortured lives are filled with guilt over broken promises and failed dreams. We all know that this man – our husband, father, and friend – tried. He committed himself to treatment, he regularly attended AA, and for a time, his disease went into remission. But finally, he died from his addiction. Many do. Alcoholism is a powerful disease. God grieves whenever anyone struggling against a spiritual disease dies of his or her addiction. So we know that God grieves with us today over the death of our loved one."

May God fill us with compassion for all those who are overcome by their addictions.

December 8

God is my protector and defender, my shelter and deliverer, in whom I trust for safety. PSALM 144:2

The psalmist presents four images of God to help us better understand the ways that God wants to work in our lives. The first is that of a protector. Like a mother lion standing guard at her lair, God protects us from danger.

And God is like a defender – one who runs defense for us, actively working to guard us from all of the forces that might hurt us.

God is also like a shelter, a place where we can go to escape bad weather, a place of security and warmth where we can rest before going on with our journey.

The final image of God is as a deliverer – one who lifts us out of the traps we make for ourselves, sets us down in a safe place, and saves us from our own destructive impulses.

These images and many others – "rock," "mother," "father," "leader," "counselor" – are incomplete if taken alone. But each is helpful as we try to relate to a God who, finally, is impossible to imagine or comprehend.

May our Creator become more real to us through these images.

December 9

I am surrounded by many troubles—too many to count! My sins have caught up with me, and I can no longer see; they are more than the hairs of my head, and I have lost my courage. PSALM 40:12

The psalmist has likely lost his courage because he has lost his balance. He can see only what is wrong with himself. He has lost all vision of what is good both in him and in his world.

The Fourth-Step inventory is intended to be a stabilizer, a way of beginning to put ourselves in balance. We discover through this process that every negative trait has a positive application, and every positive trait can be used excessively in ways that hurt ourselves and others. For instance, honesty can easily slide into rudeness or even cruelty. Having a forgiving nature can turn us into door-mats. On the other hand, self-centeredness can work to help keep us focused on ourselves and out of other people's inventories. Irresponsibility often indicates that we do not place great value on money, status or success. A thorough Fourth Step gives us a sense of equilibrium.

May our Creator help us see both the good and the bad.

December 10

God sets the time for tearing and the time for mending, the time for silence and the time for talk. ECCLESIASTES 3:7

In order to patch the worn knees on her children's jeans, the mother first tore or cut away all the frayed edges. Then she found a remnant of material and tore off a piece big enough to cover the worn spot. Only after the tearing could she begin mending. When our spirits have been damaged, when a hole is worn in our hearts, we can sometimes begin the mending process by tearing away old priorities or dreams and looking for a new vision.

The writer of Ecclesiastes combines this image with the image of silence and talking. As we seek to heal our damaged spirits, we often need a friend who will sit with us in silence and know there is nothing that needs to be said. The healing process can begin in silence – sometimes minutes or hours, sometimes days – unpressured time when reason is set aside, advice is put on the back burner, and God-talk is postponed. The time for talking will come, but if it comes too soon, it will only make the "hole" more difficult to mend.

May God bless us with times of tearing and times of silence.

December 11

If you churn milk, you get butter. If you hit someone's nose, it bleeds. If you stir up anger, you get into trouble. PROVERBS 30:33

When the writer of this proverb talks about stirring up anger, he may have had in mind the kind of behavior that makes others angry: taunting, teasing, ridiculing, back-stabbing. Clearly such behavior will get us in trouble by setting someone up to respond in kind.

The writer might also have been talking about the tendency we have to stir up our own anger. When someone hurts us, we let the hurt turn to anger and then feed the anger with memories of every other time we have let the actions of the other hurt us. The more we remember, the angrier we get, and the more justified we feel as we plan ways to get even.

We may be able to control and repress the impulse to take action on our anger, but whether we do or do not, we are in trouble. The anger, like acid, will burn us out from the inside. The best way to avoid the damage caused by anger is to go back to what it was that hurt us and tell the other, without blaming, about our pain.

May our Highest Power help us learn to handle our anger wisely.

December 12

That is when the light of the sun, the moon, and the stars will grow dim for you, and the rain clouds will never pass away. ECCLESIASTES 12:2

The writer of Ecclesiastes is describing the final stage in the aging process, that time when our senses grow dim and there is little left to hope for but a painless death. Those of us who have loved and cared for someone fading away in a nursing home or a hospital likely have a well-founded dread of ending our own days in a similar way. We do not want to be helpless or a burden to anyone.

Such feelings are honest and realistic but can be counterproductive if they keep us focused on the future, our minds filled with worst-case scenarios, our hearts dulled by fear. However, these same feelings can be transformed into energy for the day. Today is, after all, all that we know we have. There is no way to know how and when we will die. But we do know *how* to live today. And this is all that is important – a life filled with days, one after another, each one lived fully, passionately, and lovingly.

May God help us focus our energy on the day.

December 13

Sincerity and truth are what you require; fill my mind with your wisdom. Remove my sin, and I will be clean; wash me, and I will be whiter than snow.
PSALM 51:6–7

The psalmist captures the essence of a Fifth Step. What God wants from us, what God requires, is a sincere desire to see and speak the truth. Honesty is our responsibility in the process. That is all. Everything else is God's action.

As we talk, pouring out all we know about ourselves, God will fill our minds with wisdom. As we tell, we learn. As we hear ourselves speak, we discover. There is no way to predict exactly what will happen during a Fifth Step. Our Creator is at work.

God leads us into greater truth, into greater honesty, in order to help us experience the wonderful gift of total forgiveness. Our Deliverer wants to remove our sin, to wash us and make us clean. That is God's promise and God's gift. Blessed with that gift, we can enter our communities as new people, more able to love and forgive than we ever thought possible.

May God make of us new people.

December 14

If you kept a record of our sins, who could escape being condemned? But you forgive us, so that we should reverently obey you. PSALM 130:3-4

A survivor of the Holocaust commented that to forgive is to open the floodgates for the perpetuation of evil. If by forgiving we mean excusing or tolerating or even accepting the evil, then he was right. Evil must never be permitted or overlooked or excused. But that is not the way God forgives us, and neither is it the way God expects us to forgive others.

God's forgiveness of us is dependent on our repentance. That means we label past wrongdoing as absolutely unacceptable and fervently seek God's help in replacing bad attitudes and behavior with good.

What does that mean for our relationships with others? We cannot ask for nor expect forgiveness unless we are earnestly trying to change our hurtful behavior. Neither should we excuse or overlook the evil that we see around us. Forgiveness is the healing that happens in relationships and within oneself when evil is labeled as such and God's power is used to overcome it.

May we live as forgiving and forgiven people.

December 15

"Stop fighting," God says, "and know that I am God, supreme among the nations, supreme over the world."
PSALM 46:10

The woman had begun smoking when she was thirteen. In addition, she lived in an urban area with very polluted air. Because of both her own choices and her life circumstances, her lungs had gradually deteriorated until now, at age forty-five, she could hardly breathe. She quit smoking, but that was not enough. She even moved, but still her lungs did not improve. Finally, she went to a doctor, and only then did she have some hope of having her health restored.

Our relationship to God is, at times, like that of a patient to a doctor. There is only so much that we can do on our own to improve and sustain our spiritual health. Beyond that, we need the help of God who created us, knows all our needs, and wants us to come for help.

"Know that I am God." The Sixth Step clarifies the difference between the Creator and the created. We humans can cause all kinds of defects or perversions of the human spirit in ourselves and others. Only God can remove them.

May we turn our spiritual dis-ease over to our Creator.

December 16

Being cheerful keeps you healthy. It is slow death to be gloomy all the time. PROVERBS 17:22

Articles and books have been written on the value of "laugh therapy." Research shows that finding ways to lift our spirits and make ourselves laugh can help us in the battle against disease. But the laughter must be genuine, and the cheer from the soul.

When we paste on a smiling face in an attempt to cover up what we are really feeling, the mask does not help restore our health. It actually makes us worse. The mask holds the gloomy spirits inside where they can undermine our efforts to get well.

The secret, it seems, is to be honest about what we are feeling, but also to set feeling cheerful as our goal. It is not helpful to grovel in our gloom or relish our self-pity. And using our despondency to get attention is counterproductive. Not only are we hurting ourselves, but we are putting a strain on our relationships. Our gloomy spirits need to be rounded up and released so that cheer can move in.

May the Source of our being fill us with cheerful spirits.

December 17

My eyes are tired from watching for what you promised, while I ask, "When will you help me?" PSALM 119:82

The psalmist reflects a great frustration with God, but under the frustration is a sense of an intimate relationship. The writer knows God well enough to know what God's promises are. The writer has trusted his Creator and asked for help. And the writer, by implication, has an unquestioning belief that God will answer the prayer.

The psalmist also has the wonderful freedom to be frustrated and angry with God. Like a child who waits impatiently for a beloved parent to do what that parent has promised, the psalmist waits for God.

God has promised to remove our shortcomings, one at a time, if we ask. But it is easy to get impatient when we do not see enough progress in ourselves. At such times, we can go to God as a frustrated child goes to a parent and ask, "When? How long do I have to wait? Is there something else I should be doing? You promised me help. Please, I need it now." God, our loving parent, will listen and respond.

May our relationship with our Creator grow and deepen.

December 18

The start of an argument is like the first break in a dam; stop it before it goes any further. PROVERBS 17:14

The argument started over the simplest thing. In fact, when it was over, they could not remember what had started it. But now they had to try to repair the almost irreparable damage done by an hour of pouring onto each other a cesspool of old hostilities and resentments, feelings they did not even know they had.

The problem with letting an argument take its course is that there is no way of knowing how much pressure has built up behind the dam until the argument is over. Then, more often than not, the problems created by an uncontrolled flood of words are greater than the problems caused by dammed-up feelings.

It takes two to make an argument, but only one to end it. All we need to do is walk away. Tending to the pressure built up from previously inflicted hurt and pain is something to be done at another time when the floodgates can be opened carefully and the pressure released creatively.

May our Helper give us the foresight and wisdom to stop arguments before the dam breaks.

December 19

If the Lord does not build the house, the work of the builders is useless. PSALM 127:1A

When the couple first moved to the new community, they were continually impressed by the conspicuous affluence. On their evening walks they would pass one expensive, beautifully landscaped house after another. But after ten years of working closely and intimately with many of the people in the community, they came to realize that there was no correlation between the beauty of a home and the happiness of the people inside.

In one home, strife and infidelity marred the marriage. In another, teenage drug addiction twisted the relationships. Workaholism in many houses left spouses and children angry and emotionally abandoned. Religious fanaticism or dogmatism in other houses set family members against each other. . . . Houses were built and families established, but pain and loneliness were the dominant feelings.

God, the source of all love, wants to build the kind of home that allows each member to be deeply loved and fully human.

May we employ God as the builder of our home.

December 20

Foolish people don't care if they sin, but good people want to be forgiven. PROVERBS 14:9

The Eighth-Step process of making a list of all those whom we have harmed is not intended to be a breast-beating exercise in self-blame. At this stage of our spiritual recovery we no longer feel the need to punish ourselves or pour guilt over tender hearts. We have entered into a relationship with God and taken responsibility for our wrongs. We have confessed them, been forgiven, and worked at having our defects of character removed.

The task before us now is the positive task of attempting to restore broken relationships. We are "good people wanting to be forgiven." We are people who accept our power and realize that we can and have affected others. We love ourselves and want the barriers knocked down so we can love others and they can love us. We are people who know that every life is in the hands of God. Our task is not to fix, control, or repair, but to honestly love others just the way they are, letting God work with them on their own healing.

May God hold us lovingly as we explore our pasts.

December 21

Don't take it on yourself to repay a wrong. Trust the Lord, who will make it right. PROVERBS 20:22

One of the important keys to serene living is being able to turn over to God our desire for getting even. Many times in life we are wronged. There is no way that we can live in community without being hurt over and over again. There are heartless, cruel, and thoughtless people in this world, and we are often their victims. Even well-meaning people can unintentionally say or do hurtful things. The impulse to get even can totally distort our spiritual lives.

As we walk the path from Steps Six through Nine, we find the impulse for retribution, which may have dominated our lives before, fading away. As we learn to trust God to work in others' lives in the same way that God is working in us, we find ourselves loving those we once hated, praying for those we once cursed.

The release we feel is overwhelming. It becomes very apparent that we were mostly hurting ourselves by taking on the responsibility of punishing those who had hurt us. By letting God be God, we are free to be fully human.

May God free us of the need to repay a wrong.

December 22

When the Lord is pleased with you, the Lord can make your enemies into your friends. PROVERBS 16:7

There are a variety of ways that people try to get rid of enemies. Turning them into friends is certainly the most constructive. But, it is not easy, and it can be risky. In fact, problems usually come when we set about consciously trying to turn our enemies into friends. They can easily sense that they are being manipulated for our own well-being, and our efforts often produce greater animosity.

The writer of this proverb notes a different way to transform our enemies: focus on pleasing God. What does that mean in this context? Perhaps it means relying on God's power to help us repay evil with kindness, not hold onto grudges nor seek revenge, mind our own business, not attempt to change or control the other to suit us, live our own lives as lovingly and authentically as possible.

While we cannot make another cease to be our enemy and be our friend, we can set the stage for that to happen by the way we live. And God can then make it happen.

May our living reflect the love our Creator has for us and for all others.

December 23

I was on my way to the depths below, but you restored my life. PSALMS 30:3

Putting the Twelve-Step principles to work in our lives is not an instant cure nor a quick fix. But finally we reach the stage where we can look back and see the depths through which we have come. With the psalmist we can rejoice and give God credit for restoring us to life.

To live does not mean to be perfect or to have no problems. It does mean that we can now live free from our pasts and unburdened by counterproductive ways of thinking and behaving. We have learned a new way of loving ourselves and of loving others, a way that accepts rather than analyzes, admires rather than tolerates, respects rather than resents.

And, we have learned that whenever we make mistakes, we need to address them immediately, not rationalizing, not denying; but seeking to forgive ourselves, make amends, and move on with our lives. That is the way God wants us to live.

May God walk with us today.

December 24

When you stop learning, you will soon neglect what you already know. PROVERBS 19:27

We are not computers that, once programmed, never forget what they have been told to do. We are more like a car without a brake traveling up a hill. If we are not moving forward, we will surely slide backward. Old habits will return, and old addictions will eat away at our freedom. The serenity we had worked so hard to achieve will slip away from us. Worry, anxiety, and anger will take its place.

We do not always need to be moving forward in high gear. In fact, such intensity is not good for us. But we always *do* need to be moving forward – sometimes in the slow, jerky motion of first gear, sometimes at a more leisurely pace whereby we can enjoy the surroundings, and still other times with goal-oriented concentration and vigor.

The learning that gives us forward momentum comes through reading and reflection. We increase our speed when we listen and when we contemplate. Acceleration takes place when we study what we are doing and thinking, and then analyze what we are feeling.

May our Maker help us find ways to keep learning.

December 25

A country is fortunate to have a king who makes his own decisions and leaders who eat at the proper time, who control themselves and don't get drunk.
ECCLESIASTES 10:17

The model that the writer sets for leaders is one of inner strength, wisdom, and discipline. Such leaders make their own decisions, eat moderately and on a schedule, and never drink so much that their behavior or thinking is altered. Countries are indeed fortunate if their governmental officials and other leaders are persons with such self-confidence and self-control.

The writer is well aware that we are cut of one cloth—the way we conduct our personal lives will be, in one way or another, the way we conduct our professional lives. Excessiveness (being controlled by our own impulses or addictions) and lack of self-confidence (being open to control by others) are qualities that affect all aspects of our lives.

The good news is that our spiritual journey is designed specifically to help us in both these areas.

May the Source of our being continue to fill us with inner strength and wisdom.

December 26

Praise the Lord who carries our burdens day after day; it is God who delivers us. PSALM 68:19

There are two things in life that we can count on. First of all, we can and will change. Every day we are in some small and some more significant ways different people from the people we were before. These changes happen in our bodies, in our minds, in our emotions, and in our spirits. We can count on changing. *How* we change is not predictable. And because we know that we change, we can also know that others are, also, in process, never static, always growing/shrinking, living/dying. That we can count on.

The other thing we can count on is that our God does not change, and the spiritual principles on which we build our lives will remain firm. God has delivered us from all the forces within that seek to destroy us, and God will continue to do so. Our Deliverer has carried our burdens for us day after day from the moment we set them down, and we can count on never having to pick them up again. Two things we can count on: we change, God does not.

May our changeless God continue to work changes in us.

December 27

How can anyone discover what life means? It is too deep for us, too hard to understand. ECCLESIASTES 7:24

To spend our lives searching for the meaning of life is futile. While we search, our lives pass us by, and on our deathbeds we will have more questions than answers.

But "What is the meaning of life?" is a far different question from "What is the meaning of *my* life?" For the first there is no answer; for the second there are many answers, and these unfold as we live our lives boldly. They come clear as we focus ourselves on each day and ask, "What is God's will for me today?" "In what ways can I care for myself?" "In what ways can I care for others?" "How can I learn and grow?"

All of these questions have to do with hearing and responding to our callings. They require that we set out each day on a journey that will take us from the known into the unknown, and from the safe place to the place of risk, even danger. But they assume that we trust our God, a God who wants to lead us to a new land of freedom and love.

May we find meanings for our lives as we follow our Leader.

December 28

My heart aches with longing; I want to know your judgments at all times. PSALM 119:20

We are all the spiritual heirs of Eve, who saw the fruit of the forbidden tree and thought, "How wonderful it would be to be wise." We want to know the meaning, the purpose, the plan. We want to know how we fit into it all, how God sees us, what will happen to us. We struggle to know why we are the way we are and how we can change.

Somewhere, deep within, our hearts ache with longing. They quiver with infinite yearning. There is a gaping emptiness that we think knowledge will fill. But, as with Eve, the knowledge we gain only makes the yearning more intense. It only makes us aware of our need for something more.

Finally we need to realize that the answer does not come through knowledge but through assent, through saying yes to the emptiness, through embracing our infinite yearning. For it is that emptiness that connects us to all other humans. It is the yearning that propels us forward toward God.

May we embrace with tenderness our deepest yearnings.

December 29

The wicked borrow and never pay back, but good people are generous with their gifts. PSALMS 37:21

Dom Helder Camara, while working as a bishop among the poor in South America, struggled for years to change the institutional church, to make it more responsive to the needs of the poor. But as time went on, he developed a broader concept. He realized that all over the world there are people of all faiths who are working for good in whatever way they can. He called them the "Abrahamic Minority"—people on a journey to a land God will show them, people who, along the way, are blessings to all those whose lives they touch.

People involved in Twelve-Step recovery are a part of that Abrahamic Minority, a part of a network of good people all over the world who are using their gifts, whatever those gifts may be, for the betterment of humanity. These are people who know that they have been blessed so that they can be a blessing, who know that they have been given to so that they can give. These are people who are channels for the flow of love and caring around the world.

May our Creator continue to bless us so that we can be a blessing.

December 30

Useless, useless, it is all useless. But because the Philosopher was wise, he kept on teaching the people what he knew. He studied proverbs and honestly tested their truth. ECCLESIASTES 12:8–9

She had struggled with depression most of her life, going from doctor to doctor trying to find some relief. The "cures" turned out to make her problem worse. Everything seemed to her to be useless, with death the only way out. It was even hard for her friends who loved her to hold onto hope. She had done everything there was to do, and nothing seemed to help. And still she kept on, treasuring those moments when she felt good, surviving the rest, and always reaching out to others with understanding and love.

To those fortunate ones who were touched by her life, she was a model of endurance in the face of hopelessness, fortitude in the face of overwhelming inner oppression, and other-centeredness when self-absorption would have seemed justified. By simply getting up in the morning and doing what she could do, she exemplified a faith most of us never need to develop. She kept on. . . .

May God bless our lives with models of faith and endurance.

December 31

We have escaped like a bird from a hunter's trap; the trap is broken, and we are free. PSALM 124:7

Like the bird in the hunter's trap, we have been confined and oppressed by our own ways of thinking and feeling, by our own attachments and addictions, by our own dishonesty and denial. And we could not have broken the trap by ourselves. We were not strong enough.

But we turned to God our Creator, who was strong enough and who broke our old traps. And God will continue to break all the new traps we make for ourselves, if we want them broken.

God sets us free in order that we can fly unrestrained, becoming all that we are meant to be and relating to all around us with love and responsibility. Also, our Deliverer sets us free so that we can soar with the uncluttered simplicity of one carrying no burdens from the past and no baggage for the future. And whenever we need nurturing and security, we are free to nest in the assurance of our Comforter's love and providence. It is for this that we were created.

May we treasure and nurture the freedom our God has given us.

Subject Index

Abandonment
  July 9
Advice
  Jan. 5
Angels
  May 14, Oct. 8
Anger
  March 31, Sept. 24, Dec. 11, Dec. 18
Arrogance
  July 2, Nov. 30
Attachment
  Nov. 25
Calling
  Dec. 5, Dec. 27
Choices
  April 9, June 1, June 11, July 13
Contentment
  Jan. 12, Aug. 27
Controlling
  Jan. 30, Feb. 11, March 4, Aug. 23
Depression
  April 29, Dec. 30
Despair
  Feb. 29, March 5, May 22, Oct. 4
Detachment
  April 3, April 6, April 30, Oct. 17
Discipline and correction
  Feb. 22, May 9, June 13, Oct. 23
Dissatisfaction
  Jan. 22, April 20, Oct. 6
Envy
  Jan. 16, July 10, Nov. 16

Excessiveness
   April 24, Dec. 25
Excuses
   Sept. 11
Expectations
   May 2, Aug. 5, Nov. 11
Family
   June 4, Dec. 19
Fault-finding
   Jan. 13, Feb. 10, March 30, April 13, June 10, July 12, Aug. 2
Forgiveness
   Feb. 16, Aug. 13, Sept. 14, Dec. 14
Friendship
   Jan. 18, Jan. 23, March 1, March 25, Dec. 22
Generosity
   May 29
Goals
   March 8, Oct. 29
God's Intentions for us
   Jan. 1, March 28, May 3, May 12, Aug. 15, Aug. 29, Sept. 6, Sept. 8, Nov. 19, Dec. 31
God's Providence
   June 30, Aug. 6, Aug. 9, Sept. 4, Sept. 18, Sept. 22, Oct. 10, Oct. 26, Nov. 6, Nov. 24, Nov. 27
God's Silence
   Feb. 3, Oct. 2
God's Timing
   Feb. 5, March 6, July 22
Gossip
   Feb. 8, July 16, Nov. 12
Gratitude
   July 27
Honesty
   March 27, May 11, June 2, July 18, July 20

Hope
   July 7, Aug. 21, Sept. 1, Nov. 1, Nov. 2
Humility
   Feb. 27, April 11, July 1
Images of God
   Dec. 8
Inner Healing
   Jan. 11, Dec. 10
Joy
   Jan. 2, March 16, July 31, Dec. 16
Keep it simple
   July 6
Kindness
   Jan. 31, June 22
Letting Go
   Sept. 19, Oct. 20, Nov. 14
Listening
   March 14, May 30, Aug. 8, Aug. 31
Mistakes
   April 8, Oct. 21, Nov. 8
New Life
   Jan. 28, Dec. 24
Nurturing
   Dec. 1
Obedience
   July 24
One Day at a Time
   Jan. 26, Feb. 23, Feb. 25, June 25, Aug. 12, Oct. 27
   Dec. 12
Parent/child Relationships
   Feb. 28, March 24
Patience
   Sept. 16
Possessions
   June 20, June 27

Power
   March 19, May 26, Sept. 28
Powerlessness
   Aug. 3
Praise
   April 22, Nov. 17
Prayer and Meditation
   May 27, Sept. 2, Sept. 26, Nov. 28
Pride
   May 31, June 29, Aug. 26
Responsibility
   April 12, April 18, May 23, June 19, July 25, July 29, Oct. 13, Sept. 25
Revenge
   April 2, Aug. 11, Oct. 18, Nov. 4
Ridicule
   April 23, June 16
Security
   Sept. 9, Sept. 12
Self-image
   Feb. 1, March 13, May 17, Oct. 12
Self-knowledge
   March 12, Oct. 15
Serenity
   Feb. 13, Feb. 20, March 2, May 6, Oct. 1, Oct. 31
Sexuality
   May 16
Shame
   July 15
Sorrow
   April 26, April 27, Dec. 3
Suffering
   April 5, July 3, Sept. 30
Thoughts
   May 4

Tough love
  June 8
Trust
  June 26, July 28, Aug. 17, Oct. 9
Vulnerability
  Jan. 8, Feb. 6
Wisdom
  Jan. 7, Feb. 17, March 10, May 7, June 23, Aug. 20
The Power of Words
  Jan. 14, Jan. 15, March 22, June 7, Nov. 20
Worry
  May 19, Aug. 18
Yearning for God
  Nov. 9, Dec. 7, Dec. 28

Meditations on the Twelve Steps

First Step: Jan. 3, Feb. 2, March 3, April 1, May 1,
  June 3, July 4, Aug. 1, Sept. 3, Oct. 3, Nov. 3, Dec. 2
Second Step: Jan. 4, Feb. 4, March 7, April 4, May 5,
  June 5, July 5, Aug. 4, Sept. 5, Oct. 5, Nov. 5, Dec. 4
Third Step: Jan. 6, Feb. 7, March 9, April 7, May 8,
  June 6, July 8, Aug. 7, Sept. 7, Oct. 7, Nov. 7, Dec. 6
Fourth Step: Jan. 9, Jan. 10, Feb. 9, March 11, April 10,
  May 10, June 9, July 11, Aug. 10, Sept. 10, Oct. 11,
  Nov. 10, Dec. 9
Fifth Step: Jan. 17, Feb. 12, March 15, April 14,
  May 13, June 12, July 14, Aug. 14, Sept. 13, Oct. 14,
  Nov. 13, Dec. 13
Sixth Step: Jan. 19, Feb. 14, March 17, April 15,
  May 15, June 14, July 15, Aug. 16, Sept. 15, Oct. 16,
  Nov. 15, Dec. 15

Seventh Step: Jan. 20, Feb. 15, March 18, April 16, May 18, June 15, July 17, Aug. 19, Sept. 17, Oct. 19, Nov. 18, Dec. 17

Eighth Step: Jan. 21, Feb. 18, March 20, April 17, May 20, June 17, July 19, Aug. 22, Sept. 20, Oct. 22, Nov. 21, Dec. 20

Ninth Step: Jan. 24, Feb. 19, March 21, April 19, May 21, June 18, July 21, Aug. 24, Sept. 21, Oct. 24, Nov. 22, Dec. 21

Tenth Step: Jan. 25, Feb. 21, March 23, April 21, May 24, June 21, July 23, Aug. 25, Sept. 23, Oct. 25, Nov. 23, Dec. 23

Eleventh Step: Jan. 27, Feb. 24, March 26, April 25, May 25, June 24 July 26, Aug. 28, Sept. 27, Oct. 28, Nov. 26, Dec. 26

Twelfth Step: Jan. 29, Feb. 26, March 29, April 28, May 28, June 28, July 30, Aug. 30, Sept. 29, Oct. 30, Nov. 29, Dec. 29.

About the Author

MARY YLVISAKER NILSEN has written extensively in the area of chemical dependency. Her documentary novel *When a Bough Breaks: Mending the Family Tree* was published by Hazelden Educational Resources and reprinted by Harper & Row. Based on the Nilsens' own experiences with an addicted son, the book is a story of healing and hope as it follows three families through a family treatment program and relates the dramatic changes they experienced.

Mary Nilsen is also the author of a number of biblical and historical studies including one on Proverbs and another on Hebrew wisdom literature, both published by Augsburg Fortress Publishing.

In her congregation Mary facilitaties Twelve-Step groups for people seeking spiritual renewal and emotional well-being. She teaches fiction and literary non-fiction writing at the University of Iowa and is also an active public speaker. She and her husband Roy have five grown children.

Preface

The title of these meditations, *A Time for Peace*, suggests any number of images: a world where countries and peoples live without fear and in mutual respect, for example, or a family or community living without discord and dissension. But my primary intention in choosing this title was to focus on another image of peace – the peace within our own spirits, the peace from which all other peace springs.

We all know what it is to live without inner peace. Our spirits become plagued by anxieties or dissatisfactions. We find ourselves consumed by resentment, anger, envy, cravings, or fear. Whatever the destructive emotion, our sense of self becomes undermined and our power drained. We are left with little energy to love ourselves or others deeply and with abandon. In the midst of such distress, we realize there must be a better way to live, but our frenetic searchings only seem to make things worse. We finally reach that point in our lives when our yearnings for inner peace direct us to a different path, a path of spiritual recovery.

The path markings I have chosen to follow in my spiritual journey are the Twelve Steps of AA and Al-Anon. Through a clear process, these Steps lead people from bondage into freedom from those forces that would oppress their spirits. They help seekers move toward the goal of inner peace, wholeness, and a welcoming and gentle heart. These meditations reflect values and principles basic to Twelve-Step living and try to help readers keep a three-way balance in their lives — health in their relationships *with God, with others,* and *with themselves.* In addition, meditations each month on each of the Twelve Steps give readers a sense of the direction and rhythm of these Steps.

These meditations, which all spring from verses found in Psalms, Proverbs, or Ecclesiastes, were written for people seeking spiritual renewal, people who, however much they struggle with doubt, still look to the Scriptures for strength and encouragement, and call their higher power "God." I have taken some liberties in my use of this Scripture, moving freely from one translation to another (King James, from which verse numbers are taken, RSV, TEV, and JPS), and, at times, combining two translations in the same verse. In all cases I have made the human language inclusive, have eliminated masculine pronouns for God, and have sought to present a variety of images for our Creator. Together these images will help us know a God who loves us, accepts us just as we are, nurtures us day after day, and wants us to live whole, free lives.

My spiritual journey has taught me over and over again how much I need the strength, support, and encouragement of others. This writing project underscored that knowledge in very direct and practical ways. My gratitude begins with my family – my husband and children who have supported all my efforts – and extends on to my "Twelve-Step" friends. These friends have nurtured me through the years in all areas of my life. Our stories have been woven together into a fabric of love and support. I am deeply thankful to them for reading rough copies of these meditations and encouraging me to continue writing.

It is good to work with professionals who bring heart to their efforts. A very special thanks goes to my friend Nancy Jones for her clear and careful reading of final copy. Mary Ellen Carew did more than proof-read copy, she encouraged and made keen suggestions. And Judith Pendleton was friend and advisor as well as typesetter.

It has been a joy to work with my sister, Kristi

Ylvisaker—an artist who lives and paints in Sogndal, Norway—on the illustrations for the book. She took the first meditation of each month and brought her own creative interpretation to the text. Her drawings reflect a full range of human experience—vulnerability, grief, and nakedness, as well as growth, companionship, and serenity.

The project would never have been completed without the help of my dear friend Cheryl Friedman. We have walked a path of recovery together, and part of that journey has included finding ways to share our separate faiths. (She is Jewish, I am Christian.) This struggle has led us both to that space beyond the divisions history has created, a space where we can treasure those parts of our own traditions that are life-affirming, and where, together, we can worship God who is creator and sustainer of us all. She has read and carefully edited every meditation. It is our hope that these meditations will be helpful to all who look to the God of Sarah and Abraham for their deliverance and guidance.

In Peace,
Mary Y. Nilsen

Twelve Steps for Spiritual Renewal

1. *We admit* that we are powerless over *certain areas of our lives*—that our lives have become unmanageable.

2. *We come* to believe that a Power greater than ourselves *can transform us and* restore us to sanity.

3. *We make* a decision to turn our will and our lives over to the care of God, as we understand *God.*

4. *We make* a searching and fearless moral inventory of ourselves, *both our strengths and our weaknesses.*

5. *We admit* to God, to ourselves, and to another human being the exact nature of our wrongs.

6. *We become* entirely ready to have God remove all these defects of character *that prevent us from having a peace-filled life.*

7. *We humbly ask God* to remove our shortcomings.

8. *We make* a list of all persons we have harmed and become willing to make amends to them all.

9. *We make* direct amends to such persons whenever possible, except when to do so would injure them or others.

10. *We continue* to take a personal inventory and when we are wrong promptly admit it, *and when we are right, thank God for guidance.*

11. *We seek* through prayer and meditation to improve our conscious contact with God as we understand *God* praying for knowledge of *God's* will for us and the power to carry that out.

12. Having experienced a spiritual awakening as a result of these Steps, *we try* to carry this message to others and to practice these principles *for spiritual living* in all our affairs.

(reprinted and adapted with permission of AA World Service)

The Twelve Steps of Alcoholics Anonymous

1. We admitted we were powerless over alcohol – that our lives had become unmanageable. 2. Came to believe that a Power greater than ourselves could restore us to sanity. 3. Made a decision to turn our will and our lives over to the care of God as we understood Him. 4. Made a searching and fearless moral inventory of ourselves. 5. Admitted to God, to ourselves, and to another human being the exact nature of our wrongs. 6. Were entirely ready to have God remove all these defects of character. 7. Humbly asked Him to remove our shortcomings. 8. Made a list of all persons we had harmed and became willing to make amends to them all. 9. Made direct amends to such people whenever possible except when to do so would injure them or others. 10. Continued to take personal inventory and when we were wrong promptly admitted it. 11. Sought through prayer and meditation to improve our conscious contact with God as we understood Him, praying for knowledge of His will for us and the power to carry that out. 12. Having had a spiritual awakening as the result of these steps, we tried to carry this message to alcoholics and to practice these principles in all our affairs.

About the Twelve Steps

The Twelve Steps were formulated in the late 1930s by the founders of Alcoholics Anonymous as a path of recovery for those suffering from alcoholism, a mysterious, frustrating, incurable disorder that afflicts hundreds of thousands of people spanning all socioeconomic and religious categories. Where medicine, psychiatry, organized religion, and the law had failed, these Steps worked. AA groups founded on the Twelve Steps spread throughout the world giving new hope to alcoholics and those who love them.

In the past twenty years or so, there has been a mushrooming of Twelve-Step groups helping people with a wide variety of problems, not only those suffering from obvious addictions—drug addicts, gamblers, overeaters, and workaholics—but also co-dependents, persons from dysfunctional families, and persons suffering from difficult mood swings. In all cases, the Twelve Steps, combined with group support, have given relief and the hope of recovery to those afflicted.

The Twelve Steps helps such diverse people because it is much more than a recovery tool. It is a spiritual way of life, a way of approaching all struggles, of living harmoniously in relationship with ourselves, others, and God. These Steps are simply a formulation of the spiritual wisdom of the ages embodied in all the major religions of the world, but particularly obvious within the Judeo-Christian tradition. There is nothing new about the principles behind these Steps. What *is* new is that through these Steps we have been given an accessible path to help us in our spiritual journey, and through the gathering of people in Twelve-Step groups, we have been given companions to give us support along the way.

I discovered the power of the Twelve-Steps through Al-Anon during the years when we were struggling with the chemical dependency of our son. Later I wondered if these Steps could work for "ordinary" people with "ordinary" problems. I began experimenting with their use in small, religiously based groups.

And of course they did work. They worked because all people struggle with the freedom-diminishing power of attachment and addiction. We usually label someone an addict who has a chemical addiction or is perhaps a workaholic or overeater. But we are *all* enslaved – by our obsessive desire for possessions or power or by our unhealthy attachments to other people, by our rigid self-image or God-image or by our phobias, prejudices, and bigotries. We all are locked in and bound up in many areas of our lives. The Twelve Steps direct us toward a God who sets us free.

I have seen over and over again how God has been able to use this particular approach to spirituality as a way of creating in seekers a renewed spirit, an inner peace or serenity, that they never thought possible. By practicing these Steps, people find a way to tap into the empowering love of God, and their spirits are set free for the tasks of the day. Using the Twelve Steps is certainly not the only way for this to happen, but it is a way and a very good way, one that has worked for hundreds of thousands of people all over the world.

Many images come to mind when one hears the term "steps." None of these images fully captures what living the Twelve Steps is all about, but some are much more accurate than others. Thinking of the Twelve Steps as steps in a ladder or staircase is the least accurate image. This image leads us to assume that if we take each step and climb all the way to the top, we will reach a kind of spiritual perfection or happiness. If we approach these Steps with this attitude, they will lead us not to perfection, but to frustration and disillusionment.

A more helpful image would be the image underlying the statement, "I am taking steps to. . . ." We might be taking steps to get the house in order or taking steps to get our job application file updated. Whatever the goal, the steps imply a certain process, a preliminary activity that will enable us to do or be something. The Twelve Steps are something like that. We take these Steps in order to live more freely, more lovingly, more honestly. But the process is never complete. Because we struggle our whole lives with the forces both within us and outside of us that would impinge upon our freedom and serenity, we need to be continually "taking Steps."

Another image that is helpful is the image of steps in a dance. Through these Steps, we express the cadence of life, feeling and moving to the music of the Spirit. There is balance and rhythm in this song of life. Hearing its beat and treasuring its melody help us block out all the other noises that are clamoring for our attention. We can move with grace and wonderful abandon once we learn these Steps.

This is our goal. But, to learn these Steps, we must begin at the beginning, taking each Step one by one, stumbling, falling, reaching for help, and getting up again. One Step at time, one day at a time, we hold fast to God's promise to lead us as we journey out of the land of slavery, slavery to our attachments and addictions. The path is not easy, and we all must sojourn for a time in the wilderness. It is there that we discover that God does provide manna for the day. We also learn that freedom brings with it great responsibility to ourselves and to those with whom we live. We even find out that sometimes freedom is so painful and frightening that we long for the security of our addictions again. Finally, we realize how easy it is to forget the God who led us out of slavery. We must engage in constant struggle not let other attachments take the place of our dependence on our Creator.

All this we experience before we can enter our promised land—those times and places where it is possible to live life to its fullest, drinking the milk of hope and love and savoring the honey of peace.

January